THE WAY IT WAS

THE STORY OF ROGER HAMMACK AND CORYELL COUNTY

By
ROGER HAMMACK

Printed in the United States of America

ISBN: 978-1-70621-571-4

First Trade paperback edition in 2019.

Author Consultant and Editing: Michael Gray
Editor: Cathy Tesch
Cover Design: Tawni Franzen at ayaristudio.com
Text Design and Composition: Rick Soldin

All photos from the Roger Hammack Family Collection with permission.

This is a true story based on Roger Hammack's records and memory. Memories are not infallible. Please keep that in mind. The names of some characters, locations, and situations have been changed.

To Roland: I could not imagine writing this book without dedicating it to you, my brother. I still miss you tremendously. You were such a good person, helping anyone out who asked. And you were one of the best bush pilots in Alaska. You taught me how to land on glaciers and fly through some of the worst weather Alaska could dish out. I know when we meet up in heaven, you'll have some great landing strips picked out. See you soon.

~ Roger

CONTENTS

FOREWORD

The history of the great state of Texas is written by the deeds and contributions of almost two hundred years of former and current Texans. Each one has left a memorable mark on the development of our great state. These contributions can be explored in many exciting books. *The Way It Was* is one of those books.

Roger Hammack's family history dates back to 1853. From the earliest days of Coryell County, the Hammack family made their early mark on Texas as lawmen, Indian fighters, and ranchers. This book vividly describes their contributions, including Roger's continuing experiences in Coryell County both as a private citizen and as a County Constable starting in 2004. I recommend this book to anyone interested in the history of Coryell County and the contributions of those who have shared in our pride of being Texans living in Coryell County.

John E. Firth
Coryell County Judge, 2007-2018

CHAPTER ONE

June 25, 2015
Gatesville, Texas

Hammack Day had finally arrived. Each year, we held a family reunion at our ranch "It'll Do" in Coryell County. The first day was reserved for the direct descendants of my parents, and the next day added the remaining relatives. Today was Thursday, the first day, and the grill was smoking.

"Hey, Roger," Benji said, "we're ready to start."

Benji was Benji Johnson, the owner of J & M Hill Country Bar-B-Q. I always used him to cater my events. For this one, he'd spent the afternoon preparing the grill under the carport in our backyard. When he slapped the steaks on, the smell had my mouth watering. I was more than ready to eat.

"Okay, Benji," I said. "I'll round them up." I moved to the center of the carport and yelled, "Chow's on! Get it before I do or there won't be any left."

This got everyone's attention, mainly because eating lots of food was a Hammack tradition.

Benji donned a white apron and removed the foil lids from the food containers. Before he could serve the first guest, my cell phone buzzed from my back pocket. I looked at the name flashing on the screen and sighed. It was Texas Ranger Jason Bobo. We had been working on a stolen backhoe case, and he was probably calling about it.

With another sigh, I accepted the call. "Hey, how you doing there?"

"Oh, I'm doing good, Roger. Can you come down here to the office for a minute? I need to talk to you."

"Well, I'm getting ready to sit down and have supper with my family. Give me about thirty minutes."

"Naw," Jason said. "You need to come on down. Let's get this taken care of right quick."

I shook my head at the terrible timing. "All right. I'll be down."

Stepping to the food line, I said loudly, "Listen up. I need to go into town on police business. I'll be back in a few minutes, so start eating without me."

"That's the life of an honest, hardworking law enforcement official," Randy, my younger brother, said. "Who else leaves his own family reunion and all this good food to go work on stopping the bad guys?"

I held up my hand. "Hey, it's just part of the job. If it was your stolen equipment, you'd want me working 'til two in the morning, right?"

Randy nodded. "Yeah, you're right."

"We'll save you a steak," Ruth, my younger sister, added.

"Maybe," my younger brother Rodney teased.

Everyone laughed.

I left the party behind and climbed into my wife's Chrysler 300. It was still light outside, and the dashboard clock read 7:10. I fired the car up and sped into town, leaving food and family behind.

The trip to the sheriff's office took ten minutes. I walked in and didn't see Ranger Bobo anywhere. He called and said he was across the street in the Criminal Investigation Department (CID). A quick jog over and I found him.

"Hey, Jason," I said, extending my hand. "What's up? I'm missing some good food."

He shook my hand, folded his arms, and frowned. "Roger, we had a grand jury meeting over this incident in Hamilton County and they came down with an indictment. So I got a warrant for your arrest."

I blinked several times as my stomach dropped all the way to China. "For what charge?"

He handed me an indictment, tapping the thick file with his index finger. "Giving a false statement. I've been working on this case for three months."

I looked down at the document as static filled my mind, and briefly scanned it. Struggling to focus, I made out the big bold letters: "The State of Texas vs. Roger A. Hammack." They were the most sobering words I had ever read.

Heat rose to my cheeks, making the room spin a little. "This says I'm also being charged with Tampering/Fabricating Evidence. Is this a joke?" I heard myself ask.

"No. Unlike you, I'm not bluffing. And Hamilton County is looking at you for Official Oppression."

I stepped away as my eyes blurred. "I knew you guys didn't like me, but this?"

"Did you ever say that sometimes you can bluff someone?"

"No, I don't think so. What are you talking about?"

Jason moved closer. "Never mind. Let's get you to jail." When he opened the handcuffs and put them on my wrists, I thought this might be some kind of joke. Looking around for the TV cameras or my friends to jump out and surprise me, I waited. But they never appeared. As he walked me across the street in broad daylight, I knew for sure it was no gag. This was real.

He took me to the same jail I'd taken suspects to. The irony of this was not lost on me. Even the same people I knew were there to fingerprint and process me in. They patted me on the back and spoke respectfully to me. "It's okay, Roger. We'll help you get through this and back to your family." I sat on the bench, at least grateful for this kind and professional treatment. I guess it wasn't every day they arrested a Texas constable and licensed peace officer. And they made it easy for me to call my lawyer. That was nice.

After a two-and-a-half-hour computer delay, my friend Judge John Lee arrived and signed some papers. My bond had been set by a district judge at $10,000 but I was being freed on my own recognizance. This way, I wasn't out any money. Perhaps being a respectable citizen was worth something.

When they let me out of jail, it felt like the gates of hell had opened up. I was free, if only for the time being. That's when my lawyer appeared. "Roger, I just heard. Sorry I wasn't here earlier."

"Tim, these people have really got it out for me."

"Listen," he whispered, "I'm coming out to your house tomorrow morning to go over all this. Cancel everything."

That was Friday—the second day of the family reunion. *I suppose that doesn't much matter now,* I thought. "I'll be there."

"And be ready to work all day," he added.

I promised him I would. What else could I say?

A few minutes later, I pulled up to the house. The place was dark and mostly quiet, mainly because it was after ten. I walked inside and found my wife waiting.

"Benji put your food over there," she said, staring at my face. "What's wrong? Did something happen?"

I didn't reply, stumbling to my study. My wife followed and closed the door. "Roger, what's going on?"

I could barely choke out the words. "I've been indicted and arrested. I just got out of jail."

She gasped and collapsed into a chair, as speechless as me. I strode to my desk, grabbing a picture I kept prominently on display. Texas Ranger Jay Banks, my former boss and mentor, stared back at me through unseeing eyes. "Chief Banks, after what happened in Big Spring, you told me that something like this might happen to me one day," I whispered to him. "Well, it has... and boy, I sure could use some advice from you now."

CHAPTER TWO

My home office had always been a comfortable place for me to sort through mail, sit at my desk, and handle all the paperwork that came from running a ranch and a fencing business. But today the place felt like a holding cell right next to the death chamber at Huntsville. It was the last place I wanted to be.

My wife escorted Tim in. He'd done various legal work for me and was always professional and straightforward. Sometimes I'd drop into his office for a cup of coffee from his fancy drip machine and shoot the bull. His wife worked with him in the office. I'd talk to her if Tim was tied up. They were pleasant people to be around.

"Have you had breakfast?" Tim asked me, taking a seat in front of my desk.

"I wasn't hungry. Getting charged with two felonies takes away your appetite."

"I understand. I'm in the process of getting the details and evidence from the prosecutor. It'll take a few days, at least through the weekend. But meanwhile, I need to learn all the facts relating to these charges."

"Okay," I said, leaning forward and rubbing my forehead. "I can give you all that. But why are they doing this? I'm a straight-up cop. I mean, my mentor warned me years ago that others will always want to take you down, but why now? You think they might want my ranch?"

"I don't know what's going on. But rest assured, we will dig into the evidence and try to figure out what is going on."

"Okay," I said, straightening up. "Where do we start?"

Tim pulled out a legal pad. "For all my other clients, we start with the facts relating to these indictments. But I've heard a lot about your good character and integrity. I've also heard how you do things for people at your own expense and don't ask for anything in return. I know you don't like to talk about all the things you do for people, but you're facing decades in prison, so we need to start at the beginning. I want to know about your family, your background, and so forth. We'll get to these indictments later and see if we can find out what's going on. For now, let's start at the beginning—*your* beginning."

"Tim, I trust you completely, but knowing about my childhood doesn't make sense." I frowned, and he gave me a look that said I'd better start talking. With a shrug, I held up my hands. "Still, I'll do whatever you say."

Tim's mouth set into a tight, grim line. "Good. Because besides your wife, I'm pretty much the only person you can trust. Now, tell me everything about your past so I can help you in the present."

I clearly remember the day I was first inspired to go into a career in law enforcement. I was in the seventh grade, and our class was studying Texas history. I turned a page in the textbook and read the following: "In the spring of 1866, two men from Illinois by the name of Coolie and Grimes came into Coryell County and bought a herd of beef cattle about 5,000 strong and paid the foreman ten dollars a head in gold. They were a fine lot of beef cattle. None were under five years old. They took the cattle for branding out to W.W. Hammack's pens, which were about two and a half miles outside of Gatesville. They lightly burned the cattle with a road brand they needed to distinguish their cows from others along the way on the upcoming cattle drive. The brand they used for their herd was a circle G on the left side. Cattle driven up the trail were known by their road brand in those days. They planned on driving the cattle north to Kansas. One of the cow punchers (drovers) was named Taylor Hammack." The book went on to mention the Hammack name several more times, which set my mind racing. I couldn't wait to get home and ask my daddy if we were related to these people.

That evening, he told me these Hammacks were, in fact, related to us. Taylor Hammack was my great-great-uncle. Then he told me stories about W.W. Hammack, my great-great-grandfather.

"W.W. was a big rancher in Coryell County and a well-known Indian fighter. He was also a lawman—the third sheriff elected in Coryell County."

My heart soared with pride. I couldn't believe we had somebody like that in our family. I think it was that very moment when I decided to be a lawman and a rancher in Coryell County. It would be fifty years and some interesting experiences before this dream came true.

Over the next few weeks, Daddy told me more stories. At the end of the Civil War, W.W. Hammack, as sheriff of Coryell County, had to order slave owners to free their slaves and make sure it happened. His reward for doing this job was a visit from the United States Cavalry. They rode into town and promptly removed him from office as a suspected rebel sympathizer. The truth was that everyone in office had supported the South, which was why they'd been elected. But the North had won the war, so their victory allowed them to handpick their own officials.

With the sheriff's office now vacant, the cavalry appointed someone that the county residents called a carpetbagger—a person who loaded their belongings in a piece of luggage made from carpet and traveled to the South to take advantage of the losing citizens. When the carpetbagger's term was up, W.W. ran for office and was elected sheriff again.

My daddy continued to fill my head with stories about W.W., and I could hardly tear myself away from my family's history. "When W.W. was sheriff, he looked out for the people of Coryell County. He wouldn't let carpetbaggers stay in town very long. And he definitely wouldn't let the carpetbaggers take advantage of anyone in the county, especially the widows and the elderly.

"One time, a carpetbagger came into Ruby's Saloon. This man was well dressed and had a very nice wagon with a team of matched horses. As he sat down at the bar, he bragged about how much money he had and all the land he could buy. Then he started talking about a widow who lived three miles west of town. She hadn't paid her property taxes because her husband had been killed in the Civil War. She had already sold off all the cattle to keep her kids fed and was barely hanging on. The bartender knew there was about to be trouble, so he glanced at my great-great-uncle John W. Hammack, who happened to be sitting at the bar.

"Uncle John told the bartender to relax and give the man a cigar. 'Go ahead and light it for him,' J.W. said. As the man took a drag off the cigar, Uncle John stood up with his pistol and shot the cigar out of his mouth. According to the people there, the man ran from the saloon, jumped in his wagon, turned it around, and headed east as fast as those high-dollar horses could take him. Uncle John finished his whiskey and walked to the sheriff's office where he told his father, W.W., what had happened.

"W.W. knew this widow and the situation she faced. After pondering on it, W.W. gave Uncle John fifty dollars and told him to go pay the property taxes, then round up three heavy bred cows along with a small calf and take them to the Widow Powell's ranch. Uncle John did as he was told, and the widow later got a job at the general store to save the ranch."

Daddy also told me that the Hammacks first came to Coryell County in 1853 from Missouri, settling in both Coryell and Hamilton counties. W.W. Hammack chose the Fort Gates area. My great-grandfather, D.L. Hammack, settled in Ireland, Texas. He amassed 1,000 acres of land in both Coryell and Hamilton counties and ran cattle, becoming one of the better producers in the area. Besides being a great rancher, D.L. was also an Indian fighter. The history book I read said D.L. worked with posse members as they searched for Indians who raided the two counties.

Daddy and his father, Wesley Hammack, were both born on the Ireland ranch. The Ireland property stayed in the family until my father was grown. After my father's father died, the property was divided up. "As a result," my daddy said, "you have roots in both Hamilton and Coryell counties."

I began reading all I could on the Hammacks. In the mid-1850s, D.A. Hammack was elected county judge, but due to some kind of irregularity, he didn't get the position. Instead, it went to the "Know Nothing" party—a secret group of people who feared immigration and Catholics. Over the years, the Hammacks produced many elected officials in Coryell County, including two sheriffs, a constable, a district clerk, a county clerk, and several county commissioners. It was like public service was in my blood.

One day, we were sitting by the fireplace when Daddy opened a box. He pulled out an old black-and-white photo of men standing on and around a wooden gallows. People below pushed close, with several perched on the rooftops of adjacent buildings. Clearly, it was a spectacle no one wanted to miss.

"Son, this here is your great-great-uncle John W. Hammack, the sheriff of Coryell County." In the photo, Uncle John leaned against the wooden post, holding the ropes that would soon hang the condemned. "What I'm about to tell you is a family story you need to commit to heart. It starts with J. T. Mathis, a local farmer from the Union Valley community near Pidcoke. He and several other Union Valley farmers had held back their September cotton harvest. By December, the price was higher, so they loaded it up, formed a wagon train, and traveled to Gatesville to sell the cotton for cash. By noon, they headed back on the eleven-mile trip home, taking the Lampasas Road out of town.

"Late in the afternoon, they were almost home. But with the December sun long gone, it got very dark. Most of the wagon train had crossed a small stream called Riley's Branch, except for two.

One wagon belonged to J.T. Mathis. He and his young boy sat on the buckboard as he handled his mules. The moment Mathis crossed Riley's Branch, two armed highwaymen appeared on foot. The first one grabbed the mules' reins, and the other shoved a gun in Mathis's face. Both men scared the mules, who broke and ran. The mules pulled the first robber with them, causing the other to fire a shot from his pistol. The bullet just missed, skimming the back of Mathis's neck. He took the opportunity to push his son behind him and into the wagon, thus saving his life. But the first robber, still holding the mule reins, regained his footing and fired his gun directly into Mathis. It didn't look good as Mathis gained control of his wagon and took off away from the robbers."

"Did he die?" I asked.

"Hang on, son." Daddy sipped his coffee and continued. "Mr. Harvey was bringing up the rear because he had oxen pulling his wagon. He had seen the muzzle flash and knew something bad was happening. As he crossed Riley's Branch, the two highwaymen approached his wagon, but he was able to use the whip handle to strike the left side of one of the robbers' head. The man shot at Harvey but missed. The other one shot and hit Harvey in the hip, with the bullet traveling down to the base of his spine. The criminals searched Harvey for his cotton money, but he had slipped the wad from his pocket to the wagon and they couldn't find it. Thinking he was dead, the two men took off.

"The next day, poor Mathis died at home with his family around him. Thankfully, Mr. Harvey survived and was able to give a statement. J.M. Latham was the sheriff of Coryell County, and he rounded up a posse. By nightfall of the following day, he had arrested two well-known hoodlums and troublemakers: twenty-two-year-old Jim Leeper and twenty-three-year-old Ed Powell. They were charged with murder after they both admitted to being on the Lampasas Road the afternoon of the crime. They claimed they had intended to go to Leeper's uncle's house, which was eleven miles north of Gatesville, but had been drinking and ended up on the wrong road headed southwest. It didn't help their cause that Ed Powell had injuries to the left side of his head, consistent with the whip handle used by Harvey.

"Leeper and Powell told the sheriff and anyone who would listen that they were innocent. Powell's mother was rich and hired the best lawyers money could buy. This made the trial a gladiatorial affair, with defense lawyers and prosecutors fighting to the death. All the while, an angry mob of local citizens waited for a chance to kill the two men. Surrounding them were dozens of sheriff's deputies, who hoped to pull off a fair trial instead of the usual mob rule lynching. It was a fifty-fifty proposition as to the outcome: death by hanging or death by lynching. According to my grandfather, events like this were the highest drama they had back then.

"When it was over, the jury convicted the pair and sentenced them to death. But the story doesn't end there. Powell's mother paid to have the case appealed all the way up to the U.S. Supreme Court, an extremely rare move. This took a lot of time. During the appeal, your great-great-uncle John W. Hammack became the sheriff of Coryell County. With Leeper and Powell in his jail and under his protection, he got to know them both well. Each day, he listened to them swear they were innocent. But finally, the U.S. Supreme Court issued its ruling and the hanging was scheduled for September 29, 1891."

"Did Uncle John pull the lever?" I asked.

"He did. But not before Leeper and Powell told the angry crowd that they were innocent and Coryell citizens would be sorry for what they were doing. They cursed everyone there. The spectators just laughed and, minutes later, the criminals' bodies dropped and necks snapped. The crowd was silent as a slight breeze swayed the bodies back and forth. Finally, Uncle John cut the bodies down and gave them to some friends of the men."

I grabbed Daddy's arm. "Did the curse come true?"

"I can't say for sure, but I do know about two incidents that are proven facts. The first deals with Coryell County Attorney Frank

Partridge. Mr. Partridge was headed home on a train when he dis-covered his stop had been passed. Rather than waiting to get off at the next stop, he jumped from the moving car and his skull hit a train trestle, killing him instantly. They embalmed his body and shipped it back to Gatesville, where it was buried under the same huge red oak that covered Leeper and Powell."

I swallowed hard. "That's scary."

"Yeah, and the second thing I know for sure is when Uncle John was on his deathbed, he could see two men coming to get him. The men were Leeper and Powell. My father was a boy, but told me Uncle John kept saying over and over, 'I'm sorry, I had to do it. It was my job!' Even though Uncle John had been in many gun battles with Indians and killed several of them, it was these two men who showed up at the end. So, just make sure you live your life right and don't end up like Leeper and Powell."

"Don't worry, Daddy," I said. "I'm going to be a lawman."

"In that case, just make sure you take care of your citizens and help anyone in need."

"I will. I promise." I got up to go to the outhouse when he stopped me.

"And always make damn sure you get the right man. You don't want to be talking to anyone on your deathbed."

CHAPTER THREE

From the very first day I heard about my family's history in law enforcement, I knew where I was headed. I grabbed everything I could find about the profession, reading more books than the average teenager. I even read *True Detective* magazine whenever I could find it. But before I could be a cop, I'd have to grow up first and experience the bumps and bruises of life.

It all started one night in Sweetwater, Texas. The air was heavy from the recent rains of May. For some reason, my daddy, Rex Loy Hammack, Sr., and my mother, Ernestine Rebecca Tippie, eloped. Mother was only sixteen at the time.

They spent their honeymoon in Big Spring, which was probably more appealing than staying in Sweetwater. Soon after, Mother became pregnant with my brother Rex Junior. She would eventually give birth to eleven children, with me being born in the middle. The seven boys and four girls were Rex Junior, Rebecca Nell, Rosie Lee, Ronnie, Roland, Roger (me), Roberta, Randy, Ruth, Rodney, and Ralph. Perhaps because my parents were named Rex and Rebecca, they picked names that started with the letter R. The real reason remains a riddle.

In the 1930s, folks were struggling through the Great Depression. Big families were the norm, because ranchers and farmers needed everybody to work as soon as they could walk. The older kids took care of the younger ones most of the time. Also, childbirth was dangerous. Very few pregnant mothers had the advantage of doctors or drugs or birthing rooms. Luckily, my mother had the support of the hospital in Hamilton when bringing me into this world.

The 1940s arrived, and so did World War II. Daddy went off to fight. One day, we received a letter from him stating we should tell Ronnie that the G.I.s had not caught Hitler yet but were getting close. He promised to take Ronnie hunting for raccoons when he got home.

Younger brother Roland was born while Daddy was fighting in North Africa. When Daddy finally came home and walked in the door, little Roland—just two—panicked and ran under the kitchen table to hide. He had no idea who this strange man was, but he soon warmed up.

As for Daddy, he was a different man after the war. He was our father, but he was more intense and serious. Mother said he never laughed as much as he had before those horrible days in battle. And he never talked about the details of war. Instead, he'd shrug it off and talk about some funny incident. But if you looked deep into his eyes, you could catch a permanent shade of sadness. Over time, I learned to never bring the subject up.

My first home was in Hamilton, a small, friendly Texas town. We had a little farm with big rocks and a small cliff perched over my bedroom. I found it hard to sleep for fear of one of the massive boulders rolling down and crushing me to death. Fortunately, I managed to escape that fate.

Because there was little work available, Daddy used the G.I. Bill to purchase a little farm in Fairy, Texas. We raised sheep and hogs. For crops, Daddy grew cotton and planted wheat in the fall, harvesting it in the summer before planting cotton again. Most of the hogs were sold, with a few butchered and stored in our smokehouse for later consumption. When Mother wanted to cook some, we just grabbed a hunk from the storage box. It was good eating.

The kids who were big enough had household and farming jobs. Even though I was just three, it was my job to get the sheep penned at night. That turned out to be more of a job than one would think. Mother trained me how to handle those sheep, but it was like herding cats. Sheep make up their own minds, changing frequently. Mother hated the sheep. She complained that they were the dumbest animals God ever created (perhaps something went wrong with their design). To help me, she'd drive them to the pen. As soon as I opened the gate, where food, water, and safety awaited, they'd turn and run in the opposite direction. I guess Mother didn't know the trick of putting a little corn in a bucket. They would've followed her anywhere.

The tiny house we lived in had no electricity or running water. It did have an outhouse with flies and other critters. We used magazine pages and newspapers for toilet paper. Sometimes we had soft corn cobs too.

Living in a large family, sharing hand-me-downs, and working hard proved to be a challenging life. We played, we fought, we worked, and we tolerated each other. I would say love, but you know how brothers are about acknowledging that.

I had some good memories from that place. Mother, on the other hand, felt different. One afternoon, I asked her if she ever missed that ranch in Fairy. She was very quick to say, "Heavens no! Your stubborn, pig-headed father pulled us out of Hamilton where we had running water, electricity, and other conveniences. In Fairy, all I did was work from daylight 'til dark six days a week." She hated that place with a passion.

Somehow, Mother convinced Daddy to move. She probably locked him in the outhouse for a couple days. That would break anybody.

With work in the area limited, Daddy searched hard for a job. He lucked into this little place in Alabama, which changed our lives.

I was still three when we moved to Mobile, Alabama. Daddy had landed a civil service job at an ammunition dump. We lived out in the country on other people's farms or nurseries, and would take care of the land in place of rent. All of us worked around the farm, tending to the animals or hoeing weeds. To me, it wasn't really work—more fun than anything else.

One time, Daddy was plowing a field when he came to the house out of breath. "Grab a stick and come on," he said to me and Roland. I thought a monster was coming, so I grabbed the biggest stick I could find and ran behind him. Once we reached the field, I saw rats everywhere. It was a moving rat carpet. No horror movie could compare.

We beat the rats as much as we could, but there were too many. At one point, they turned their teeth to us and we had to be careful not to get bit. After that, we decided to get some cats.

Gene and Rosie were an elderly black couple who also lived on the farm. Their grandparents had been slaves in the same area. Gene and Rosie were hardworking, good people, and I got along with them really well. In the spring, Rosie would make us kites using old newspapers and glue made from flour and water. Those kites lasted all summer.

One day, Daddy shot a possum that was after our chickens and took it to their house. Rosie set to work and cooked it up, bringing it back to our house when it was done. I can still see that possum floating in a pan of grease, its head hanging over one side and its snakelike tail over the other. I assume someone in our family ate it. I know I didn't.

While we lived on the farm, Randy was just a toddler. During the day, he would take a nap in his crib and, incredibly, a chicken would come through the window and lay an egg right next to him. I believe he bonded with that chicken, because he's been able to raise any kind of bird all his life.

We stayed in Alabama for about six or seven years before Daddy was transferred. We had to leave our friends behind, including Gene and Rosie and that crazy chicken. I never heard what happened to the couple, but I'm pretty sure that chicken ended up in Rosie's pan.

We moved to Supply, North Carolina, when I was in the fourth grade. It was a tiny town near the coast with nothing but a feedstore and three or four houses. We, of course, found a place in the country to live, with plenty of room to roam.

Roland, Ronnie, and I had lots of fun fishing. I would save my lunch money to buy bait—a pound of shrimp for a dime.

When I was twelve years old and going into the fifth grade, a tobacco farmer came by looking for some help. He had two fields. Ronnie, Roland, and I raised our hands and took the job. Roland was thirteen and Ronnie was fifteen. We worked two days a week cropping the tobacco leaves (pulling the leaves off). It was a five-day process that required the largest leaves from the bottom of the stalk to be picked on Monday, and the rest picked on Friday. By having four days for the remaining leaves to grow, the tobacco ripened.

We worked from daylight to dark. Roland and I were paid $3 a day because we worked in the shed, hanging the leaves in the barn. Ronnie worked in the field, pulling the two bottom leaves off the tobacco stalk, before loading them in a drag-behind skid (a trailer on skids). He'd drive an old mule pulling the laden skid to a shady spot underneath the shed, and we'd unload the leaves onto a large bench. Roland and I stood to either side of a stringer, with a woman who worked there. We'd pick up two leaves at a time, alternating between handing them to her. She'd tie the leaves to a four-foot pole as fast as we handed them to her. When the string was full, we'd carry it up to the top of the barn and place it on a drying rack. There it stayed until the entire string had dried.

I can't lie—the work was hard. That black tobacco juice stained our hands. Whenever I ate a sandwich, the bitter taste seeped into the bread and made everything nasty. Sadly, that's when I became addicted to nicotine. I remember the first time I lit a cigarette, I was hooked. It took a long time for me to quit.

We accomplished all the tobacco work during the summer. I don't remember how many days we worked, but we didn't get paid until the owner sold his tobacco at the never-ending auctions in Charlotte, Charleston, and Raleigh. There, tobacco buyers dropped off their crop for auctioneers to sell. When the farmer sold his tobacco, he came by and paid us. I remember to this day the feel of that $53 in my hands. I'd never seen so much money. Roland got the same as I did, while Ronnie made $70. But it was time for school and we needed to get school clothes. With eleven kids in the family, Roland, Ronnie, and I handed our money to Mother. She was able to buy school clothes for all of us. To this day, that's one of my proudest/ biggest accomplishments. And I never regretted working all summer for money I couldn't keep. That's just the way it was.

We stayed in North Carolina for about three years until Daddy was able to get a transfer to Texas. I was excited about going back. I didn't know much about exactly where we were going, but it was Texas. How could anyone *not* get excited?

CHAPTER FOUR

During the summer of 1958, our family rolled into Big Spring ready for a new adventure. I didn't know much about the location, other than Texas was a land of heat and dust and real lawmen.

Daddy's new civil service job made him a fireman at Webb Air Force Base. To help with expenses, Mother worked at the base as a clerk, even though her number one job was raising and caring for her eleven children.

I was going into junior high—the seventh grade—and felt really excited. We had never lived in a large town like Big Spring; one with an exploding population of 35,000 and out of control crime.

Up to this point, we'd always lived in the country. Out there, crime was nonexistent. But in Big Spring, life was very different. Sure, we could walk to the store and get a soda. But we'd be putting our life on the line.

We quickly learned there were lots of murders. Armed robberies were as frequent as break-ins, and usually the robbers killed the gas station attendant. Each morning revealed the latest business destroyed from an overnight break-in. Plus, there were never-ending episodes of fist fights, knife fights, and all kinds of other crimes. It was a wild and dangerous town.

As a teenager, all I knew of bad guys was what I'd learned from watching the Lone Ranger, Cisco Kid, and Roy Rogers on TV. These heroes would round up criminals and haul them to jail—shooting the pistols from their hands, of course. The violence in Big Spring was so pervasive that the need for strong, dedicated law enforcement was obvious. Where were the lawmen I'd seen so often on television? Surely, they could clean this place up. There had to be a solution.

That fall, I started junior high school. There were at least 2,000 students crammed into one old building. I was stunned. I'd never been around that many people in my life. Unfortunately, the town's violence spread to the students, too. Two boys in my class got in a knife fight down at the movie theater. One died and the other was charged with murder. They were only thirteen. I couldn't believe something like that happened. It still bothers me to this day.

After school, I'd have to walk a dangerous two miles to get home. I was always scared something would happen.

One day, I happened to pick up the newspaper and a big, bold headline caught my eye. "Jay Banks, a retired Captain of the Texas Rangers, comes to Big Spring as Chief of Police." I'd heard a lot about the Texas Rangers, but had never seen one. I felt real proud someone so important was coming to our town. But unlike my TV heroes, he didn't ride in on a horse. He took the train instead.

It was June 15, 1960, when the townspeople met Chief Banks at the station and showed him around town, helping him get situated. He didn't disappoint.

Within two months, Chief Banks and his cleaned up/highly motivated crew had caught the criminals responsible for robbing the gas stations and killing attendants. The whole town breathed a sigh of relief.

While reading his daily reports of crime, I became more determined than ever to become an officer of the law. I was going to protect and help people no matter what.

Eventually, we moved to the south side of Big Spring. This put me in the Forsan High School district, named after the four sands drilled through before hitting oil. Even at $3 a barrel, Forsan was a very rich school district.

When I entered the ninth grade, the freshman boys had to go through an initiation. We wore dresses and ran through a gauntlet of upper-class boys, each holding a belt and hitting us good. When I saw Roland, he didn't use his belt on me. In our family, that's the way it was.

I finished high school in 1964 and attended college. I realized real quick I couldn't afford the tuition. People always say, "There's a time and place for everything, and it's called college." Maybe that's true, but college takes money and I had very little. Back then, there were very few opportunities to get student loans like they have today. With money tight, I needed to find a career path that could sustain me for the rest of my life.

At the time, I had a 1964 Ford Ranchero. This was the first vehicle I'd ever bought brand new. I was making a $60 a month payment, which was a lot of money in the sixties. I worked all through high school and after graduation to keep making the payments on that car.

After high school, I worked in an auto body shop and made fifty cents an hour. My job was to write estimates for damaged vehicles. I lived at home to save money. Before long, I found a job working for an independent insurance adjusting company. I went to a special school in Dallas to obtain my adjusting license and did this for a while, until I began to feel restless. In 1964, at nineteen, I decided to try my luck out on the West Coast—a land of new opportunities.

I loaded up my car and drove through New Mexico into Nevada, heading straight to the Las Vegas Strip. There weren't any big parking garages back then, so I found a spot on the curb and walked right into a casino. I spent a few hours there, losing some dollars in the slot machines. After a while, I decided I'd tested my luck enough. It was time to move on.

I left Las Vegas and drove up to Reno. The country around Reno was painted with beautiful trees and mountains, and looked nothing like Las Vegas. I circled around and drove to California, where my brother Ronnie lived. I stayed with him until I could find a job.

It didn't take long, especially since I wasn't picky. I was hired by a service company to be a janitor at the Lockheed Missiles and Space Center. I worked really hard, maintaining a conscientious attitude while keeping the toilets clean. One day, a person with Lockheed came over to me and said, "I've been watching you. You have an impressive work ethic."

"Well, I try my best," I said.

He stared at me for a couple moments. "How would you like to go to work for Lockheed?"

"Man," I said, grinning, "I'd love it."

He handed me an application and got me hired. Suddenly, I was making $4.60 an hour working in the machine shop for the space department. With forty hours a week, I was doing great!

After a few years in California, I turned twenty-one. I'd gone on a couple dates with a girl when she brought Mary Wiley over to my apartment. As soon as I saw Mary, I knew right off she was the one for me.

She was beautiful, with a perfect hourglass figure. And she was very smart. She looked like the perfect schoolteacher. I set my cap and went after her, winning her heart before she even realized what was happening.

Mary and I didn't date very long—three weeks. We headed for Reno, Nevada, and got married on February 18, 1967. Fifty-one years later, I can honestly say that she's the best thing that ever happened to me.

Mary and I lived in my apartment for a little while. I made good money. Life was great, but I wanted more. I wanted to buy a house. When I told Mary, she was scared to death. She hated debt, especially what we'd have to borrow. However, I calmed her down with a nice three-bedroom house in San Jose, paying a modest $11,000. Today, it would be worth more than $400,000.

Our first daughter, Regina, was born a year later. Holding her stirred my soul. I wanted to provide her with a great life. So I pondered my future. I enjoyed working for Lockheed, but I still had a strong sense of right and wrong. Plus, I'd always wanted to get into law enforcement. With the cost of living spiraling higher in California and crime on the rise, I just had to get out.

My decision was made for me. One afternoon, I had just hoed some weeds in my garden and dropped the grubbing hoe to get a glass of tea. When I came back, the hoe was gone. That was the end of California for me.

I talked to Mary and she agreed to move back to Texas. There, I hoped a law enforcement job awaited me. And, if I was really lucky, I'd find a ranch and be like my forefathers.

It didn't take long to sell our house. I gave notice to Lockheed and left the machine shop and all those space parts behind. They'd just have to launch all those Apollos without me.

After cashing my last check on Friday, we loaded up the car the next day and took off for Big Spring, Texas.

It was 1969 when I started working in a body shop again. But all I could think about was being in law enforcement. Finally, enough was enough. "Today's the day," I said.

I went down to the Big Spring Police Department and asked to speak with Chief Jay Banks. He had been there nine long years and clamped down hard on crime. I had read everything I could find about him. There was a lot of material. I figured I had an edge.

A clerk pointed me to his office and I took a deep breath as I went in. The second I saw him, I was shocked. He was a big man, probably six-foot-six and close to 300 pounds. Huge! He was so much larger than life that he made me look like a little ant. And he oozed confidence.

I shook his massive paw and said, "Chief, I'm here to ask you for a job as a police officer. I've kept my nose clean all these years because I've wanted to be in law enforcement. It's my life's dream. Ever since you came to Big Spring in 1960, I've wanted to work for you. In fact, I've read every single thing I can about you. It's like I know you. Really, it would be a great honor to work for you. Will you please give me the opportunity?"

He moved in close and looked down at me, grumbling something about the fact that they were going to have a test in a day or so. After he'd studied my thin frame, he said, "We'll get an application for you."

He took me to a clerk, where I sat down and filled out the application. I left the law enforcement experience section blank, hoping Chief Banks would overlook that since I was just beginning my career. He snatched the completed form from my hand, studied it closely, and said, "Come in and take the test. We'll see what happens."

I thanked him as I left, feeling like I was on Cloud Nine.

Two days later, I came back and took the test with two other men. That's when I discovered there were only two openings. I bore down and did the best I could, hoping it was enough.

It wasn't.

The other two guys got hired, leaving me to continue my work at the body shop. I kicked myself and muttered, "Well, that was my chance and I didn't get it. I washed out."

Five days later, I answered a knock on my door and found a police officer, Sgt. John Scott, standing there. "Are you Roger Hammack?" he asked, his right hand on his pistol.

"Uhh… yes," I replied nervously.

"Chief Banks wants to see you."

My eyes grew as big as saucers and my voice cracked. "What does he want to see me about? I ain't done nothing."

His brow furrowed. "You applied for a job, didn't you? Well, he wants to talk to you about it."

Hearing those words, I just lit up. I couldn't believe it. My heart jumped into my throat.

I went down there and walked into Chief Banks's office. I was nervous, of course. He no longer grumbled but spoke softly. "Roger, we have an opening here starting next Wednesday. If you still want the job, you can have it."

"You bet!" I blurted out. "Chief, thank you! Thank you! Thank you!"

He shook my hand forever because I didn't want to let go. "Okay. Get with Sgt. Scott and find you a uniform." He looked me up and down. "And see if he can find one that'll fit you."

They gave me a couple of uniforms, but each one hung on me like they were made for a giant. At that time, I weighed only about 140 pounds, standing barely five-eight. I soon learned I was the smallest person on the force.

After digging through the bins, Sgt. Scott found the smallest uniforms they had. I raced to my grandmother, Nellie Tippie, a seamstress in Big Spring. "Grandma, is there any way you can make these uniforms fit me?"

She looked them over. "Well, give them to me and I'll see what I can do."

A few days later, I had two uniforms that fit perfectly. When I pinned on my badge, I felt like a million bucks. I was as proud as I could be. Then I felt for my gun. I didn't have one. That was the only piece of equipment I had to provide myself.

Unfortunately, the move to Texas had cost me a lot. I was so broke I couldn't even afford to buy a pistol. Daddy stepped in and went to a pawn shop, where he found a nickel-plated Model 10 Smith and Wesson .38 Special. I still have that gun today.

Once I put on my uniform and holstered my new gun, I was set. I reported to work on Wednesday and was sworn in by Sgt. Scott. That was it. No academy. No special training. No nothing.

"Time to punch in," they said. I was now an official Texas law enforcement officer. My dream had come true.

My lawyer raised his hand for me to stop. "So, let me see what I have so far." He flipped through his legal pad. "Your family has been in Coryell County since the beginning. They've been lawmen, clerks, and sheriffs. You admired Chief Jay Banks and wanted to be just like him, maybe even a Texas Ranger."

"That's right," I said.

"Hmm. You've got a good reputation. Maybe they're looking to pull you down a bit."

I frowned. "I don't see why, but nothing would surprise me at this point."

Tim tilted his cup. "Any chance I could get a refill? We're going to be here awhile."

"Sure," I said, calling Mary to bring in a fresh pot.

Tim poured himself a cup and took a sip. After he sighed, he flipped to a fresh page and motioned for me to continue.

CHAPTER FIVE

Even though I was a real police officer, that didn't mean Chief Banks was going to let me wander the streets of Big Spring alone. He told me that as a new officer, I'd have to ride around with a senior patrolman for a few days, a few weeks, or a few months. "Whatever it takes for us to feel confident you know what you're doing," he explained. After that, I'd be working on my own, since the days of two cops patrolling in a single car were long gone.

I carried a clipboard and climbed into the squad car, barely believing I was about to get paid for being a cop. In fact, it was one of the proudest moments of my life.

Bill Rogers was the senior patrolman assigned to train me. Our shift started at midnight and ended at eight. I settled in for a long, but exciting night.

We patrolled the downtown area for several hours seeing nothing out of the ordinary. Around two in the morning, Bill said, "Hey, let's go see if we can find us some rabbits."

He steered the car up South Mountain until we spotted some rabbits. As we stood on the side of the road shooting, I assumed this was some kind of ritual for the new guy. Or maybe they just wanted to see if I could handle a weapon. If that was the case, they had no doubts when we were done. I easily outshot Bill.

As we blasted away, I grew nervous. "Hey, Bill. What if somebody calls dispatch about the shooting out here?"

He laughed. "Who are they going to call? Us? If they do, we'll go check it out."

That's the way it went on my first night. Not much action and a whole lot of boredom.

Over time, Bill and I became good friends. Chief Banks rotated me around with other patrolmen too. One of them was Gary Wells. I'd been working two weeks when we received a call about a hit-and-run traffic accident at the city park. Since no injuries had been reported, we leisurely cruised over to the scene.

When we arrived, we started gathering the information. Apparently, one vehicle had sideswiped another and left the scene. About ten minutes into our investigation, a car came zipping by. The victims grabbed me and started pointing. "Hell, that's it! That's the car that hit us right there."

The car slowed, seemingly studying us before taking off. Gary and I jumped into our car, hit the lights and siren, and laid rubber after them. The culprit had a good head start and a fast car, but we gained with each turn. We chased the car through downtown Big Spring until Gary drew close enough to ram him. He tried knocking him off the road but couldn't do it. With no other options, we kept chasing the car until we hit it so many times the hood of our old Ford bowed up and sent steam spewing from the engine.

Still, Gary kept the pedal down. "No way you're getting away," he muttered, his jaw clenched.

Seconds later, the criminal made a left turn. When he did, Gary undercut him. With my door closest to the side of the fleeing vehicle, I caught a glimpse of the driver—a young male, maybe twenty. We raced along side-by-side, swapping paint, urging our car to get ahead so we could hit his left front panel and end the chase. But this guy had souped up his car—a two-door '57 Ford Fairlane. He was going to be a tough out.

Our radio blasted through the chaos, a voice cutting through the roar of our car's engine. "Stop that car any way you can! He's going to kill someone."

It was the sergeant. He and the captain were in a car right behind us, watching everything. Acting out of sheer instinct, I reached below my seat and grabbed a tire thumper I kept there for just such a moment. Then, like something out of a movie, I leaned out the window and swung the club at the suspect. The first strike managed to connect with his face, splattering blood all over his dashboard and windshield. I watched as his car careened into the only tree on that entire street. The tree ripped off the right side of the car, turning wooden splinters and metal into missiles. Gary put our car into a slide, just missing the Ford and the tree. Before we came to a stop, I jumped from my window and raced to the car, pinning the suspect to the ground. As I handcuffed him, he came to—woozy but conscious.

"I'll be damned!" the captain yelled, running up and slapping me on the back. "And all without a shot fired."

That was important in a big city. Firing guns sent bullets everywhere—into stores, houses, and possibly people. Using your gun was always a last resort.

The sergeant came up after the captain and congratulated us for a job well done. He assessed the damage. Our car was still drivable, but it had clearly been through a war. The Ford Fairlane was totaled. Eventually, the suspect would pay to repair our car while serving a lengthy jail sentence. He wasn't a hardened criminal—just some kid with money who'd decided to run.

That incident set me on a path to making a good name for myself with the other patrolmen, as well as my supervisors. The cops I worked with relaxed. I could tell they trusted me now.

One night, I showed up to work and saw Chief Banks. "Roger, can I talk to you a second?"

"Sure," I replied, a little nervous about what he might want.

He escorted me to his office and closed the door. "I've been studying your work and talking to the men. They feel like you can handle yourself. So I'm going to let you get a car and run your own calls. Understand?"

My chest swelled with excitement. "Yes, Chief."

"Now, listen here," he said, leaning over the desk. "I tell every man who works for me the same thing. It's time to tell you."

I pulled out my notepad, but he stopped me. "You don't need that. I want you to just concentrate on my words. Okay?"

"Yes, Chief."

He placed his palms flat on the desk. "Each policeman has two cowardly tools at his disposal. The first is to tell the victim that this is a civil matter and no report is needed. That way, you can simply walk away having done nothing. The second is to tell them it's a domestic dispute. You can leave the woman with the man so she'll get beaten again."

He raised a finger, pointing straight at me. "In my department, we don't do that. We *work*! That means investigations and reports and arrests. It's difficult and time-consuming. But we're here to serve and protect. We serve by helping people out. We protect by catching the bad guys and keeping them from hurting more citizens. Sure, it's always easier to walk away from a problem. But in my department, we're not afraid of problems. We serve and protect. Got that?"

"Yes, Chief," I replied. "Serve and protect. I'll do both."

"Good, because I want you to stay with it and be a good cop. And just know that I'll be watching."

His words rang in my ears for years. And from that moment on, I dedicated myself to doing exactly what he'd ordered: serve and protect.

I had been with the Big Spring Police Department for a month, always working the night shift. I loved that time because that's where the action was. It seemed as soon as the clock struck midnight, the problems started.

It was a hot Tuesday night. The air was heavy as I cruised around looking for problems. Suddenly, patrolman Len Williams put a call through the radio requesting assistance. He had spotted a burglar running from a beer joint and was proceeding on foot after the suspect. Since I was just a few blocks away, I responded immediately.

When I got there, I saw Len struggling with a large man. Len had been on top, but the man was too strong. Now, the burglar had gotten on top of him and was about to severely injure Len—if not kill him. With no other option, I leapt from my car and ran fast. I was a few feet away when the man turned his head to see me coming. This was it. I dove straight at him, crashing my shoulder into his neck. The blow tilted this large man to the side like a ship about to capsize.

Len used this to his advantage, pushing hard to force the man over on his side. As fists flew from every direction, Len and I took a beating. But we gave one too. Finally, we struggled to get the big man handcuffed. With the suspect secure, we licked our wounds, trying to catch our breath.

More squad cars arrived and helped Len get the suspect to jail. With that over, I resumed my patrol.

At the end of the shift, I dropped by the station and heard everyone talking about what had happened. Len had spread the story around, saying, "Boy, that Roger has got your back. Don't ever think he doesn't. He'll be there for you no matter what. You should've seen him take that guy right off me."

My colleagues had already studied that mountain of a man in jail and were amazed. Even Chief Banks grinned. He actually looked *smaller* than this guy. And everyone wondered out loud what would've happened to Len if I had not been there. Luckily, this incident added to my growing reputation as a solid cop.

During those first years, we worked eight-hour shifts, six days a week. My off day was Thursday nights but I didn't really enjoy it.

That's why I'd tell my wife I was going down to the police station to see what was going on. I'd find one of the patrolmen who didn't have anybody to ride with and work that shift with him. In fact, I loved my job so much, I wanted to learn all I could. For the first year or two, I don't remember ever taking a day off.

From the beginning, it seemed like I had a knack for law enforcement. I patrolled the streets at night with a spotlight, looking through store windows and downtown businesses. I caught several burglars inside buildings. I even helped catch armed robbers and murderers. My arrests were adding up.

For me, life was rocking along just fine. My daughter, Regina, enjoyed Big Spring and so did Mary. And I was thrilled with my career. Then a big problem hit the city.

Burglaries exploded overnight. Every night, some criminal broke into a store or business, stealing everything they could. At times, it seemed like a riot was going on—where people break plate-glass windows and climb in to pillage the place. The only problem was, there weren't any riots. Just stealing. The situation was dire.

The townspeople, led by the business owners, stormed into Chief Banks's office and demanded action. The Chief emerged from the meeting and called everyone to the station.

"I need some volunteers to work the night shift so we can catch these guys."

I raised my hand because I'd been working a new evening shift, getting off at 9:30 p.m. Chief Banks slotted me to start that night. After more men volunteered, the Chief released us to rest up.

Outside, I found myself standing next to Jack Boyd. He was a crusty old sergeant and a heck of a man. Jack treated everyone as close friends. He was always there if you needed help, and he wanted to be the first one through the door. Sgt. Boyd ran toward trouble, not away from it.

I told him, "Sergeant, we're gonna catch those burglars tonight."

He shook his head and grimaced. "Roger, I sure hope we do."

I was ordered to patrol the north side of Big Spring, which was the rough side of town. Riding with me was Ben Montanez, a young guy learning the ropes. As we made our rounds, we came to a beer joint called the Red Barn. I eased the car to a stop and aimed my spotlight at the entrance. Sure enough, the door had been kicked in. I moved the car closer and saw beer cans stacked up right beside the door. It was obvious we had come upon the burglars, spooking them back inside. I picked up the radio and called Sgt. Jack Boyd, explaining the situation.

"Hang loose and stay in the car," Sgt. Boyd said. "I'll be there. Don't go in until I arrive."

We waited and waited. When he finally pulled up, he and I crept to the door and had a look inside. Slowly and methodically, we searched the beer joint, finding no one. As we walked back to the car, I pulled him close and whispered, "Sergeant, I feel like they're still inside because that beer is right by the door. I don't think they'd go off and leave that. And we didn't see anybody run out. I'm pretty sure they're still in there."

Sgt. Boyd rubbed his grizzled jaw. "Okay, Roger, let's go."

He grabbed his twelve-gauge shotgun and loaded it with double-ought buckshot. I had my pistol and pulled it out. With our senses heightened, we went back in and searched the building again, from top to bottom. Like the first time, we didn't find a soul.

Back at the car, Sgt. Boyd called headquarters and told them the burglars had gotten away but we would secure the place. About that time, I saw my partner standing around. I said, "Ben, come on. Look at all this beer stacked up here. I don't think those guys have left this building. They couldn't have gotten out. They *must* be here."

For a third time, I went back inside and looked for the mysterious burglars. As the hairs on the back of my neck stood up, my gut kicked in. All of a sudden, I saw something out of the corner of my eye. I turned around and spotted a body wedged behind a corner booth. It was a tiny space, but the skinny young punk—probably sixteen or seventeen—had somehow squeezed in.

I whipped my flashlight around and the beam hit his eyes. Pointing my gun at him, I yelled, "Stand up, now!"

As he stood up, he dropped a six-inch-long hunting knife he'd been holding as a dagger. When I heard the knife hit the ground, I breathed easier. We handcuffed the kid and took him outside.

In law enforcement, it doesn't take long to learn that the most dangerous people are young juveniles—teenagers. The reason for this is that they are scared to death. They greatly fear arrest and jail because they know it's the end of their world. An older person who has been convicted several times will just throw up his hands and walk out. He knows he can take a chance on working the system. The juveniles, on the other hand, will kill you in a heartbeat. They're dangerous because they're so scared.

When Sgt. Boyd saw us, his eyes widened. He hugged me and said, "I sure didn't think they were in there. You did good."

About that same time, one of the other detectives who was working with us called in and said, "Hey, there's a carload of kids hiding down this road."

The detective had been driving our way when he saw a car loaded with apparent "friends" of the first burglar. Sgt. Boyd said, "Roger, go ahead and take that kid to jail and book him in. We'll set up and watch these other guys to see what's going on. Just leave everything as it is, with the door kicked in and the beer stacked there."

We followed his instructions, taking the long way to jail to avoid these suspects seeing their friend arrested. Sure enough, that car pulled up and six of the accomplices jumped out and ran inside the building. They started stealing everything they could. The detective, Bill Lee, and his partner rounded them up and brought them in, making the first night's haul seven burglars.

Through some later forensics, that hunting knife the kid was going to stick through my ribs turned out to be part of a haul from a previous burglary the Howard County Sheriff's Department was working. When the suspects' fingerprints matched up on all the crime scenes, we discovered that it was these kids who'd been breaking into everything and causing a world of trouble. Incredibly, we shut the entire thing down that first night.

A few weeks later, Chief Banks hand-delivered a nice letter to me, recognizing my actions that night. I enjoyed reading it and showing the letter to Mary, but truthfully, the most important and self-fulfilling part centered on the job itself. My work in law enforcement was the right fit for me. There was no other way to say it. I really loved doing my job. But I also knew no matter how many attaboys I got, it only took one screw-up to lose everything. If I was to keep my job and stay alive, I'd have to be at the top of my game each time I punched in for a shift. Otherwise, it could be my last.

With the burglars stopped, the armed robberies picked up. They were hard to handle and even harder to solve, because these bad guys didn't like to leave witnesses. We did joint raids with the FBI and struggled to get control of the chaos. It was an embarrassment that Big Spring was rated as one of the most dangerous cities per population density in the entire United States. Chief Banks was determined to keep plugging away.

One day, I showed up for my shift and he pulled me into his office. "Roger, I'm going to send you to the police academy."

"Gosh, Chief, I'd like to stay and help you catch these guys."

"And I'd like to have you here, but it's a requirement for you to keep your peace officer's license. You must go within your first year, so I have to send you. It's only four weeks, which in this town can mean life and death for some folks. Still, it's a requirement."

I thought he was done, but he motioned for me to stay. "Look, you've already learned the street knowledge from the senior patrolman. Now you'll learn some book knowledge. It will help you be a better patrolman. Just don't let it change the person you are. I have enough of those guys."

"Don't worry, it won't."

"Just come back to me the way you are, but a lot smarter."

I smiled. "I'll do my best, Chief."

"You always do," he muttered as I left his office.

CHAPTER SIX

Before I left for the academy, the men gave me a sendoff. We had lunch at a local diner where I listened to stories of their training. Many of them had been grandfathered in and never attended the academy. The others tried to convince me I'd be swallowed whole and never make it out again. Thankfully, it wasn't like that.

The police academy was located at Texas A&M University at College Station. It was pretty straightforward. There were hours and hours of classroom study. We learned the law. We went out into the field and investigated traffic crime scenes. We filled out endless reams of paperwork. This was followed by several days on the firing range. I picked up tips on how to place each round on center mass, praying I'd never have to shoot someone. But if I did, I wanted to be ready.

When my four weeks ended, I was a certified senior patrolman. Now, it was time to get back to Big Spring and catch some bad guys.

One night, I was out patrolling and happened to pass by a little restaurant. I noticed two long-haired individuals (we called them hippies) leaning against an old Ford truck. They were gesturing and talking to two redneck-looking guys, nervously looking around for anyone watching. Since it was extremely rare to see hippies and rednecks hanging out together, my gut told me to check it out.

Rather than drive up on them, I pulled around the corner and waited for the men to split up. I eased the squad car to a stop but left the engine running. Suddenly, the two rednecks jumped in their truck and drove off.

Quickly analyzing the situation, I decided to leave the hippies alone and follow the rednecks. I cruised behind the truck for a while until they committed a traffic violation. Then I pulled up close and flashed the blues, stopping them on the shoulder of the road.

My academy instructor had said I was good at sniffing out crime. As I exited my car, I put my sniffer on full alert.

Using a calm approach, I politely asked the two rednecks to get out of the car so I could talk to them. I asked a few innocuous questions about stolen liquor before asking if I could look inside their vehicle. They glanced at each other and, to my surprise, said yes.

During this time, there wasn't a big problem with drugs. Sure, we heard about marijuana, LSD, and heroin. But it was all new to me. I had never seen an illegal drug in my life. That's why the two rednecks were shocked when I reached inside the truck and opened the glovebox. There, I spotted a half-open matchbox with a green leafy substance inside it. I assumed it was marijuana, even though I had learned the drug was sold in Ziplock baggies or something called a lid.

The two suspects danced around until I relaxed them by saying I just wanted to check out something. Once I had them convinced, I got inside my patrol car and called for backup. The reason I did this was simple: I had only one pair of handcuffs. The last thing I wanted to do was handcuff one guy and have the other resist. So, when the on-duty sergeant, Don Thorpe, arrived, I was relieved.

Don came over and checked out my haul. Fortunately, he'd called for more help on the way over, because the captain and two other patrol cars showed up right behind him. I followed Sgt. Thorpe to his vehicle and held out the matchbox. "I don't know for sure, but I think this might be marijuana."

"Really?" he said, inspecting it. "I ain't never seen it before."

I chuckled. "Well, I haven't seen it either. But I think that's what it is."

Sgt. Thorpe and I took the subjects to the police department, where we booked and charged them with suspicion of possession of marijuana. After a sample tested positive, I was told that I'd just made the first arrest in the area for possession of drugs—*any* drugs. I also learned that the penalty for possession of marijuana was a felony, punishable by two years to life in the state penitentiary. The size and amount didn't matter. That's how serious Texas was about drugs.

After this, Sgt. Thorpe and I became great friends. He nicknamed me Kilo and that stuck for a while. A few years later, he died in an automobile accident.

A week after the arrest, Chief Banks called me into his office. He started off telling me about the Police Chiefs Association, an organization of police chiefs from all over Texas. Chief Banks was acting president at that time. Recently, they had held several meetings concerning the problems with drugs. Apparently, several cities were struggling with the problem. The association had concluded that the best way to stop the flow of drugs was to take police officers and have them work undercover in the targeted towns. Chief Banks asked me bluntly, "Roger, would you be willing to give undercover work a try?"

I said yes before he could finish his sentence.

"We have funded the position of an undercover officer for Big Spring. The way it's going to work is we'll pay you to work in the target town and receive one of their officers in return to work undercover here. Understand?"

"Yes, Chief. I promise I'll do my best."

"I'm sure you will... *Kilo*."

I smiled and got up to leave.

"Oh, and take a couple weeks off to relax. This undercover work will be twenty-four/seven. You won't have a day off. When you get back, I'll tell you where you're going."

I raced home and made plans to go to California. I knew Mary wanted to visit her family, and I'd have time to grow a beard and let my hair go. When I got back from California, I looked pretty shabby. Even Mary was stunned at my transformation.

Chief Banks told me no one else in Big Spring knew where I was going. He dropped me off at the Midland airport and gave me an envelope with a ticket and instructions. When I saw the word Dallas on the ticket, I swallowed hard. I was going to the big leagues.

I arrived in Dallas and used the instructions to take a cab to a Holiday Inn on the North Freeway. There, I was met by a Texas Ranger named Red Arnold, who took me to another man. This guy was the district attorney of Sulphur Springs. I didn't understand why he was here, but Red told me to get in the D.A.'s car and go with him. When we cleared the Dallas city limits, he told me we were going to Sulphur Springs—in the heart of East Texas—where my real assignment was.

Silently, I was relieved. I didn't much like starting out my undercover career in a place as massive as Dallas. I figured Sulphur Springs had to be similar to Big Spring. After all, they shared a fondness of springs.

When we arrived, he drove me around the town for a while, helping get me familiar with the area. He stopped near a little hole-in-the-wall pizza joint where he thought the drug dealers hung out. He also showed me the motel where I'd be staying. After the tour, he took me to pick up a vehicle and handed me a wallet full of cash—all hundreds. I'd never seen so much money in my life. It added up to $1,500.

"Listen, Roger," he said. "You need this money to look like a big spender. I want you to spend it around. Be conspicuous. And don't worry about the money, because we've already written it off as an expense for the undercover work."

I took the money and nodded. Then he added, "I've never worked with you, so I don't know how you are as a cop. But let me tell you this: If you find a drug dealer but can't get the evidence we need to arrest him, it's real easy to make a case by just lying and making stuff up. It happens all the time. The only time problems pop up is when you're wrong and the guy wasn't who you thought he was. So when we lie, we become no different than the criminals we're trying to catch. We're putting a lot of money and time into this. If it pays off, great. If not, that's okay too. But whatever you do, don't lie."

He picked up a napkin he had in the car. "Our freedom is like this napkin. There's only so much of it available. When a cop lies, it's like a little piece of our freedom is ripped off and it never comes back. Do you follow me?"

I did. His speech made me feel better about this operation. It took the pressure off.

I drove to a convenience store, where I used a hundred-dollar bill to buy a few things. I flashed the clerk a quick glimpse of my wad too. As I left the store, I didn't know it, but the store manager was calling the police chief, telling him that some long-haired hippie bought cigarettes with hundred-dollar bills. I almost lost my cover because the police department didn't know I was working in their town. I only found this out a few days later when the district attorney checked in on me.

That evening, I ventured out on my first trip to the pizza place. It was one of those places with aspirations for restaurant status but somehow found itself stuck on the bottom rung of a fast food dive. It even had a drive-thru window. You had to yell your order because none of the outside speakers worked. The place seemed like a cross between an abandoned motel and a construction shack ready for bull-dozing. Even the light bulbs in the sign couldn't spell Pizza. Instead, they flashed a big red Pi—a.

I found a booth with a nice view of the place and ordered a small pizza. While it was being cooked, I played some pinball. I also kept feeding money into the jukebox, listening to some hardcore '60s hits. Soon, I noticed some long-haired kids who looked like drug users, or at least marijuana smokers. But I wasn't going to jump to conclusions. It was just my experience that certain motorcycle clubs wore leather jackets. Certain peace/flower-power communal groups maintained a common look with jewelry, headbands, long hair, beards, colorful shirts with fringe, low-hung bellbottom jeans, and flip-flops. There may have also been some users and dealers of other drugs I had never heard of hanging around too, but I couldn't be sure. I just spent my time trying to get a feel for the place and the people there.

During the first hour, I tried to act like I fit in. Yet it was obvious that despite my shaggy hair and scruffy beard, I was an outsider. I left after a few more hours without making contact with anyone, deciding to try my luck again the next day.

The following day, I came back and went through the same routine. Despite lots of pizza and pinball, I still couldn't establish any type of contact with anybody. If I tried to talk to someone, they just brushed me off and walked away. I didn't want to push things, so I just kept coming back and casually hanging out.

The next day was Saturday. I went to the pizza place late in the afternoon and found the joint crowded. I started going through the same routine—playing pinball and feeding money into the jukebox. I was sitting at a table by myself eating a piece of pizza when three redneck cowboys walked in the door. They seemed to be looking for trouble.

I watched as they pushed the long-haired hippies around. That's when I saw my chance to make contact. Mustering up my courage, I walked over to one of the male hippies. He had plaited pigtails hanging down over a green shirt with yellow flowers. I whispered to him, "I'll whip that big cowboy if you'll keep the other cowboys off me." The hippie looked me up and down, grinned out the side of his mouth as though he doubted my ability, and said, "Right on, man."

I walked over to the big cowboy and bumped into him, slurring my words as I said, "Well, excuse me."

That got his attention. He stepped back and sized me up, deciding he could make quick work of me. "Why don't we just step outside?" he said.

I nodded and muttered, "Sure, I'm right behind you."

As we went out the door, I got the first blow in and he went down. I had him on the pavement and was hitting him in the face. About that time, the other two cowboys got me down and were kicking the daylights out of me. All three of them bashed my ribs and face. Through foggy eyes, I saw blood splattering everywhere. Unfortunately, it was all mine.

I could only lie there, staring at all that blood. I couldn't get another blow in and had to take the pain. So much for the hippies helping me. They just sat there, watching the little dude get the crap stomped out of him.

About that time, the city police arrived and started sorting out the situation. The cowboys jumped up and dusted themselves off, acting like nothing had happened. The hippies made moves to walk away when one of the policemen picked my carcass up and dragged me over to the car. He looked me over and asked, "What's going on here?"

I shrugged nonchalantly. "Aw, hell, nothing much. I just fell and busted my head."

One of the officers said, "Come on, tell us what happened."

"Don't worry about it," I yelled, loud enough for everyone to hear. "I'll take care of it."

The police officer grabbed my shoulder. "You'd better not cause any trouble here. Understand?"

"Yeah," I said, smirking. "I promise it won't be here, but I'll handle it." Then I tried to calm things down by saying everything was groovy.

The police officer asked for my name and driver's license. "Dickey," I told him, matching the phony license Sgt. Pete Stone, the Big Spring Police Department's fingerprint technician, had made for me. It had no photo, just a Big Spring address.

He grew agitated at all the blood I was spilling on his patrol car. Another officer leaned in and asked if I wanted to go to the hospital. "No thanks," I replied.

The police wanted to arrest me and the cowboys, but I knew they couldn't arrest only one person for fighting. They had to arrest two. Since I wasn't pointing the finger at anyone, they had to let me go.

As one of the police officers helped me over to my car, I walked past the cowboys and looked at them with a crooked grin. They got the message that I wasn't done with them. Then I shrugged to the confused hippies.

While driving back to my motel, I noticed that I had chipped a tooth. I smiled, knowing I now had some common ground with the hippies. I'd soon find out if they felt the same way about me. If so, I might be able to find out if they were dealing drugs. I grinned painfully and limped to my room, confident my plan was starting to work.

Once I locked myself in the room, I washed my face and looked in the mirror. What a mess! My face looked like hamburger meat, and my lower lip was cracked and bleeding. I tried to comb out my shaggy brown hair, but it was caked with blood. My body groaned as I sat down in a chair. It felt like I'd been dragged behind a truck on a gravel road.

Since it was after 10 p.m., I decided to go to bed and sleep as tenderly as I could. To my surprise, I slept until ten the next night. When I finally woke up, I could barely climb out of bed. Every inch of my body hurt. I was in so much pain that I didn't know if I could even walk. And I was starving—but I didn't want a pizza.

I cleaned up as best I could and eased into my car, driving outside of town to a truck stop. There, I literally drank a pot of coffee. For a midnight dinner, I downed a massive chicken fried steak. I couldn't get enough food.

The waitress asked what had happened to my face and I replied that I'd fallen from my truck while tying down a load. She shook her head in disbelief and said, "Dickey, I know you got into it with those cowboys." I blinked several times, amazed she knew my name since I hadn't told her. Obviously, my undercover persona was getting around town.

When she returned to refill my cup, she whispered, "Did you shoot their car up?"

Her question stunned me but I tried to remain cool. Apparently, someone had fired a gun at their car. I knew it wasn't me, but I was undercover. My answer would have to be deceptive. "Did I hit anybody?" I asked. "I was trying to kill them."

She looked around. "No, but you put a lot of holes in their car."

I shook my head. "Well, I'll be a son of a gun. Do you think they'll be coming around here again? I'd sure like to finish it."

"No, I don't think they'll ever come around here again as long as you're in town."

I finished my meal and went back to the motel, smiling as best as I could with a busted lip and throbbing ribs. Things were right on track.

I got back to the room and tried to straighten it up. I remembered the blood on the sheets and towels after I had cleaned up from the fight and wondered if the cleaning lady had told the manager or called the police. If so, who knew where that would lead?

I was unpacking my bags when I found my three-year-old's pajamas in with my clothes. Regina had put them in my suitcase because she'd wanted to go with me. It was heartbreaking, making me a little sad.

I picked up the pajamas and smelled them. Then I laid them on the bed, sleeping next to them. Despite my pain and the pot of coffee, her little gift allowed me to sleep like a baby.

The next morning, I stared at those little pajamas lying there on the bed. It made me realize the seriousness of the job. I knew it was a dangerous mission, but I loved my family so much I just knew I'd get the job done. Chief Banks and the district attorney were counting on me.

I located my weapon and checked the action. Because I was undercover, carrying a gun wasn't an option. It might blow my cover or get me arrested. Satisfied, I shoved it back under the mattress and hoped the cleaning lady wasn't so thorough.

The next day, Monday, around three in the afternoon, I gathered up my courage and went back to the pizza place. When I went inside, I noticed the same crowd of long-haired hippies. My face was still cut up badly and it hurt. I could feel my chipped tooth and the swollen lip with my tongue as I walked up to order a pizza. Instead of playing the pinball machine, I sat down at a booth and tried to relax. That's when I noticed a skinny little hippie girl with waist-length dirty-blonde hair, no makeup, and flip-flops. She was with two more hippies in a booth. I assumed if they weren't working on a Monday, maybe they were dealing drugs.

I had been there no more than five minutes when the girl came over and sat down in my booth across from me. She said her name was Kathy. Her speech and mannerisms gave me the impression that at one point she'd been to college in California. "I was there on Saturday when you got in that fight," she said, playfully twirling a strand of her hair. "One of those cowboys was my boyfriend, but we aren't dating anymore."

"You're making a smart move by dumping that loser," I said.

About that time, the other hippies came over to my booth. Before I knew it, the booths around me were full. One hippie confirmed that the cowboys' truck had been shot up with holes. "Did you shoot those bastards' car?"

I smiled and said nothing, letting them check out my chipped tooth.

"I knew it!" a hippie in another booth said.

Magically, I'd found some long-lost friends. To celebrate, I bought all the pizza they could eat. We played the jukebox and talked for five hours. The first song Kathy played was "Snowbird," because that was the song I had played the most.

When I got ready to leave, Kathy came up close to me. "Are you going to be back tomorrow?"

I nodded.

"I'll be back too," she said with a twinkle in her eye.

I shrugged. "See ya tomorrow."

The next day, I had a surprise meeting with the district attorney. He had left me a note to meet him on a deserted road. There, he told me about flashing the cash around and the buzz I'd created with the fight. He asked if I had made contact.

"Yeah. Yesterday was the first time. I think I have a fish hooked. I'll take it easy and reel it in carefully."

I gave him more details and concluded the meeting, driving back to the pizza joint. Sure enough, there was Kathy with two male hippies sitting at a booth. Again, it seemed like they didn't have any possible work schedule or other commitments. I figured they had to be dealing drugs to support their lifestyle. I also wondered if they ate anything other than pizza.

As I sat down in the booth and started to drink my soda, Kathy walked over. "Let's go get some beer," she said, tilting her head toward the door.

The second she said that, I reevaluated my observations. Did she want romance instead of a drug deal? Was I chasing a dead end?

I agreed and we went out to my car. "Where do you want to go?" I asked.

"Oh, just some little town close by. Hopkins County is dry."

I slid into the front seat and cranked up the engine. Kathy took her time but slid in next to me. Out of nowhere, the two male hippies she'd been with opened the back doors and climbed in. Seeing my apprehension, Kathy said, "Is it okay for them to go with us?"

I sized them up, unsure of where this was heading. At least the romance angle was eliminated.

"Yeah," I replied. Really, I had no choice if I didn't want to blow my cover.

I drove for over an hour and we still weren't there. A sprawling lake appeared with a long bridge over it. As my tires endlessly clicked off the expansion joints, I started getting a bad feeling. This might be a setup.

Carefully and slowly, I reached down between my legs to get the gun I always kept underneath my seat. When my fingers returned unrewarded, I remembered I had left it in the room under the mattress. I was undercover. I couldn't carry a weapon. I wanted to slap my thigh but couldn't.

With every mile, I was sure I was driving to the spot where they would kill me. They would probably have me dig my own grave. When the hippie behind me tapped my shoulder and said to turn down a dirt road, I tried not to think about Regina's pajamas. At least Mary would get those back when they shipped my body home.

Hopefully.

CHAPTER SEVEN

"Turn here," the hippie behind me said.

I snuck a peek in the rearview mirror to see if he had a gun to the back of my head. From what I could see, he didn't.

A store with a sign that read "Beer and Wine" came into view. I breathed a silent sigh of relief. *Maybe this will all be okay.*

I pulled in front and saw that the store was connected to a restaurant. This was my chance to ease the situation and see where it was headed.

"Hey, guys," I said, "how about we eat some lunch? I'm hungry."

"I don't have any money with me," Kathy said, lying through her teeth.

"No problem," I said. "I'll buy for everyone."

Suddenly, the mood changed. Everyone was happy with ol' Roger... I mean Dickey.

We ordered the food and I got to know the two male hippies. They seemed afraid of the guy who'd taken on three big redneck cowboys. They were no threat.

After lunch, I bought some beer and we drove back to my motel room to drink some of it. The funny thing is, I never liked beer. That's why I could barely finish one and had to nurse a second.

We talked about life in Sulphur Springs, of which I knew nothing. I made it clear I was from another town, which seemed to fascinate them. Several hours later, I was their regular friend.

With the day fading, I decided to take the two male hippies back to their car at the pizza joint, leaving Kathy at the room. I told them

I'd see them the next day and came back to my motel room for the night to find Kathy asleep on the bed. The words of the district attorney knocked around my head. "Absolutely no hanky-panky with the girls. If you do, you'll ruin the entire case." I was also married, so I didn't need that warning. Still, I had a sticky situation. I didn't want to blow my cover, since a legitimate drug buyer would be pawing the clothes off this young girl. What to do?

I decided the best course of action was to sleep fully clothed on top of the covers next to her. So I quietly lowered myself to the bed and was about to rest my head on the pillow when I spotted Regina's pajamas. If Kathy saw those, she'd question my background. Maybe she'd already seen them and wasn't going to say anything. Who knew? Checking to make sure her eyes were closed, I snatched up the pajamas and held them next to me as I drifted off to sleep.

I learned later these hippie girls looked at me as a sort of friend/ protector. They felt safe with me, like sleeping with the Lone Ranger or Batman. No way those guys would try anything. I could only imagine what would have happened to Kathy if I *had* been a real-life drug addict.

The next morning, she woke refreshed and unmolested. I freshened up and suggested we go to the truck stop for breakfast. Kathy agreed, and we took off.

I was hungry when we sat down in a booth and ordered coffee. It was the same waitress from before. When Kathy got up to make a phone call, the waitress brought her face down to my level and whispered, "Coffee is free when you come here, Dickey." I was amazed how many women a man could get in Sulphur Springs by simply taking an ass whipping.

Kathy eventually returned and began a stare-off with the waitress. I hoped they wouldn't start a fight over me. They'd be sorely disappointed when they found out I had a wife and a child. Oh, and I was a cop who could arrest one of them.

We stocked up on pancakes, scrambled eggs, and bacon, savoring each bite. While we ate, Kathy asked me my name and where I was from. I blinked several times, not believing that throughout this entire time, I'd never said my name, or she hadn't heard the rumors. I had to think this was another test.

"My name is Dickey," I said. "I live in Big Spring."

"What are you doing so far from home?"

This was it. The big question. The moment of truth. My next words would decide the fate of some of these hippies.

I leaned over closer to her and started telling my story. "I work for a madam out in West Texas. This lady needs some marijuana for the girls working there. It helps keep them calm—and from going back and forth to town to look for it on their own."

"Why doesn't she just go to town and buy it for them?"

I hadn't covered that angle. I had to think fast. "The male supplier operates a similar business as hers, and my boss can't stand supporting his business. She's sent me east to find some."

"Why did you come all the way here instead of stopping in Fort Worth, or maybe Dallas?"

Another excellent question. I guess when you're operating a business that can put you in prison for life, you grow some brains.

"Because one of the girls is from Sulphur Springs. She said she'd bought some at this pizza place. Rather than stumble all through Texas looking for some pot and risk running into a cop, I decided to drive here and see what happens."

She looked down at her food, saying nothing.

"Can you help me, Kathy?"

"I don't know," she said.

"That's okay, because either way, I leave in a few days with or without success. But if I find a steady supplier, I'll be back every month to pick up another order."

Her eyes lit up at the mention of a steady cash flow. "You know, Dickey, I think I can help you." She went to the payphone again. When she came back, she told me to be at the pizza place that afternoon at four. I was relieved and excited. She assured me that one of her friends said to tell me not to worry about anything. He had me covered.

"Do you want to get some beer to celebrate?" I asked.

"Sure," she said with a smile as big as Texas. And why not? She didn't have to be into work... like, ever!

We drove across the county and bought a case of beer. Again, it took an hour both ways. When we got back, I stopped at a convenience store and flashed some money around again. I figured I'd send another message to the D.A.

I made it to the pizza place early and found Kathy sitting in a booth sipping on a soda. We drank a Coke together and played the jukebox. I was pretty sure that in the drug world, Kathy and I were going steady.

At four sharp, a young man came in and sat down beside Kathy. He shook my hand, studying me intently. "I understand you're looking for something to smoke."

"Yes," I said. "About twelve to fifteen lids of grass to take back to a woman in West Texas."

He asked me to detail the story I had told Kathy, and I did. When I was done, I sipped my soda, waiting to see what he would decide.

"I think I can get you what you need in a few days."

"Good," I said, "because a few days is all I have left."

He smirked. "I don't care if you're a narc or not—because if you are, I'll just kill you."

I smiled back. "Don't worry. No one has to die simply because my employer needs some smoke for her girls."

That put him at ease. He set a price of $10 a lid (or ounce). I agreed, and we were done. Of course, I was thinking to myself that this guy was a real punk. Wouldn't his parents be disappointed when he was arrested?

He said he'd meet me outside town in an hour and the girl knew where it was. I guess the two days he needed had just been a lie.

Kathy and I drove back to my motel. I told her I wanted to get a jacket because the nights were getting chilly. I went inside and wrapped my pistol in the jacket, placing it in the backseat of the car. Then we drove out of town, taking a frontage road to the middle of nowhere. It was a perfect place to murder an undercover cop.

I parked behind the punk's vehicle. I had a briefcase on the floor-board behind my front seat filled with a few things for the road like candy and cigarettes. Slipping my gun inside, I carried the briefcase to the meeting. After my earlier scare in the car, I figured no investigation was worth dying for.

Standing next to our cars, we both scanned the horizon for any spies. Satisfied that no one was around, the hippie moved close and handed me a bag. I looked inside, holding up some weed so I could put my nose to it.

"Man, this smells good," I said emphatically. With such a limited experience with drugs, he could have put oregano in there and I wouldn't have known the difference. Thank God it was actually pot.

He showed me fifteen lids and demanded $150. I peeled off the bills and handed him the cash. While he greedily counted the money, I shoved the pot in my briefcase. Once he had put the money away and was paying attention, I told him I needed this amount every month. He said to contact Kathy and we'd be fine.

Kathy and I hopped back in the car and headed to the motel. "You know, I have to see a cousin in Fort Worth," I told her. "I'm going to head back, but I sure can't wait to see you again."

She giggled and touched my arm. "I can't wait for you to come back too. I don't have a boyfriend, you know."

I gave her my best sultry look and dropped her off at the pizza joint. Then I made a call to the district attorney.

The next morning, the district attorney came and picked me up. We drove to a deserted area and I started talking. After I laid out the details for him, he wanted me to go after another dealer. I told him the story I used to make this first case wouldn't work because I'd already told them I was leaving the next day. Besides, I'd already taken one ass whipping. I needed a break. He understood, and told me to drive to his office at 3:00 p.m.

Back at the motel, I quickly packed up. I wanted to catch a bite to eat before I got out of town, so I went to a new place rather than the truck stop or the pizza joint. There was no sense in being spotted there and having to answer questions.

At three, I showed up at the district attorney's office. In the conference room, I handed him the briefcase full of marijuana. He emptied the contraband on the table and inspected it. A thin man in a knit shirt and some slacks walked through the door, carrying a commercial camera. The district attorney patted him on the back and said, "Dickey, this guy is from the newspaper. He's going take a photograph of the lids you purchased."

The photographer stood behind me and took a picture of my back along with the stash of marijuana. I was concerned about this picture, but said nothing.

After the photographer left, I talked to the district attorney for some time and made sure no charges would be filed against Kathy. I told him that the deal couldn't have been made without her help and hoped if she needed help in the future, he'd be there for her. He agreed.

The district attorney's investigator loaded me in his car and headed for Dallas. We talked a great deal during the ride back. He said several times how proud he and the district attorney were of my work. I asked if he'd send me three copies of the newspaper article. A couple days later, I received them along with a generous letter from the district attorney thanking me.

The investigator dropped me off at Love Field Airport. As I walked to the door, I noticed a statue of a Texas Ranger and walked up to it. I did a double take, dumbfounded as I realized the statue was of Captain Jay Banks, my current boss. What a crazy feeling to see a statue of your boss in an airport.

After a short flight, I landed in Midland to find Mary and Regina waiting for me. Regina gave me a big hug as pride filled my chest.

"How did it go?" Mary asked.

"You know, one day I'll write a book and you can read all about it." I showed her my chipped tooth. "But know this: it was an adventure. I'll remember this trip for a long, long time."

We went to eat and I told her I wasn't going into work for a few days since no one knew I was back in town. "But listen, honey. I need you to keep a close eye on everything for a while. There was this snot-nosed punk in that little town who swore to kill me if I turned out to be a narc."

Mary's eyes widened. "What the hell did you get into?"

I just shrugged. "Oh, not much more than usual for a lawman."

Two days later, I called the dispatcher and asked what shift I was scheduled to work. She told me the evening shift. I told her I'd see her then.

As soon as I walked into the police department, Chief Banks asked me to come into his office. "I heard from the district attorney," he said. "He told me what an excellent job you did. I told him how happy I am to have you working for me. And I am."

I thanked him and said I had to get to work. Outside his office, Sgt. Boyd slapped me on the back and said, "Good to have you back, Roger. I heard some rednecks gave you a bit of a hard time."

I grinned, showing them my souvenir. "I tried my best to put up with their hillbilly ways. Guess I just wasn't smooth enough for their tastes."

We all laughed, because everyone knew the story went a lot deeper. The guys wanted a few stories and I obliged. Then we geared up to catch some bad guys.

I got back to patrolling, never thinking much of what I'd done until my tongue touched that chipped tooth. I'd smile and think back to that ass whipping I'd taken. Still, I felt apprehensive about that dealer. You never knew about a criminal. Some of those guys had long memories.

For a good many nights, I watched my rearview mirror. If I saw a vehicle from Hopkins County, I'd pull it over and check to see if it was anyone I recognized. Luckily, no one ever came looking for me. And later, I learned the dealer pled guilty and went to prison. So that was the end of that.

Today, it seems strange that the penalty for possession of a small amount of marijuana was so harsh back then. Sometimes I think that if we'd kept the stricter penalties for drugs, we wouldn't have the problems we have today.

Almost every town in the United States has a major drug problem. Many people die each day from drug overdoses—even more than from automobile accidents. Drugs will remain a problem for a long time to come.

About a week after I got back in town, Chief Banks called me into his office and asked if I knew a girl named Kathy from Sulphur Springs.

"Yes," I replied, swallowing hard. "She helped me out on a drug buy while I was there. Why?"

He handed me a letter in a plastic bag addressed to him from Kathy. I read the pages and learned she wanted me to write to her because she desperately wanted to get out of Sulphur Springs. She was planning to move to Colorado City (about thirty miles from Big Spring) to be closer to me. I guess she had gotten attached to Dickey. I felt really bad for her, because I hadn't done anything to lead her on. I guess she hadn't experienced many guys who treated her with some sort of respect.

"Did anything else go on?" the Chief asked, his eyebrows forming a deep V.

"Of course not. But I'm going to have to explain all this to my wife, for Pete's sake."

"Hold off until I have the letter analyzed for fingerprints. When I'm done, you can have it to show your wife. Just make sure you show it to her early in the day so you can have time to look for a motel room to stay in."

We chuckled and left it at that. A few weeks later, I had the letter and showed Mary. She completely trusted me. In fact, she shook her head and said she felt sorry for that poor girl. It was a sad life for someone to live. Hopefully, she turned it around.

CHAPTER EIGHT

After that pizza adventure, I had more confidence. I worked another undercover assignment in the Dallas area—the big leagues. As usual, I had to remember there was no backup. Nobody was physically or electronically tailing me. I was truly on my own. And I wasn't checking in with my superiors to let them know where I was headed. If something bad happened and they buried me deep, this was the line that came next: "Listen, Mary, maybe Roger will turn up one day."

Yeah.

Although I only made a few drug buys in Dallas, I managed to secure enough information for the local detectives to make some raids. I worked a few more undercover assignments that year, but without much success. The Police Association felt we weren't making enough progress, so they scaled us way back.

When I was back on regular duty in Big Spring, I attended a seminar on drugs. I met state troopers who also worked undercover narcotics. We got to talking and they said that two other officers in Texas had gotten severely messed up on drugs. One of them had their drink spiked with LSD, messing the officer up for life. The other officer had done nothing more than handle some LSD he had purchased. Apparently, he'd held it in his hand long enough for it to be absorbed into the blood system. He was also messed up a lot, but would recover. I felt bad for them.

At this seminar, all of the undercover officers looked the part—long hair and beards—and they could really speak the lingo. One night, we sat around drinking beer and telling wild stories. About one in the morning, I managed to make it back to my room, where I slept until checkout time. At least I learned a lot.

I'd been back in Big Spring for about three weeks when the detective captain called me into his office. He said they were sending me on another assignment to Dallas. Before, I'd been targeting marijuana dealers. Now, I'd be going after bigger fish—dealers of LSD and heroin. These dudes carried weapons and weren't afraid to use them.

When I got ready to leave Big Spring, the captain slipped me my contact in Dallas, the place and time. It just so happened that my rendezvous point was the same Texas Ranger statue at the airport. I'd never said anything to the Chief, but the news stories had made it clear it was modeled after him.

I met my contact and drove to a motel, where I checked in and waited. They said they'd be back with the informant.

A few hours later, my contact brought me a vehicle with an informant inside. The two detectives pulled me aside and gave me some advice. One of them said, "This is a very rough area you're going to. Lots of drugs and dangerous people. Really, we should just fence it off and let the criminals eat themselves."

I blinked a few times to make sure I'd heard that. Then he continued. "Don't trust this informant. In fact, carry your weapon with you at all times. If you get into a bad situation and have to use it, just serve up some .38 caliber warrants to the bad guys and walk away. Go find a phone and contact us. We'll chalk it up as another drug deal gone bad. Understand?"

I told them I did. They said if I needed anything, just call. Otherwise, they'd see me in a couple days.

As they left, the other detective handed me $500 and glanced at the informant. "Good luck," he said. "You're gonna need it."

The informant's name was Sherri. She looked like the typical drug addict and was probably high on LSD. I know, because we sat in the motel room talking so we could get to know each other. This was critical. We needed to fool the targets into believing we knew each other well. I could tell that if it came to her having to match up a storyline with mine, I might as well pull out my .38 special and start shooting, making sure to save one bullet for me.

While we talked, she was insistent that I take some LSD. I joked and said I preferred battery acid.

"Have you done that too?" she asked. "Isn't it great?" (I had no way of knowing that years later, some smart guy would use battery acid to make a new drug: crystal meth.)

At dark, we took my car and went driving around. She pointed out an apartment building and we stopped.

"You follow me," she said as she staggered to an outside staircase.

Walking up, I got a bad feeling about this setup. I can't say why, but I felt like I was going to my death. I touched my .38 to make sure it was still there. It was.

Sherri knocked on the door and it opened slowly, a mysterious face checking us out. The exterior light mounted next to the door illuminated our faces, casting a shadow over the person inside. We passed the test and went inside.

When the door closed behind me, the room was dark. The only light came from the hallway. My eyes hadn't adjusted yet, so all I saw were dark faces sitting around the room. When I was finally able to focus, I wished we could go back to the darkness. The characters from the small towns I'd been working in were choir boys compared to these predators. Their faces displayed all the years they'd been buying and selling drugs, perhaps doing time in prison. A few of them were definitely high on something. For the second time in a minute, I felt my .38 to make sure it was there. It was.

"Have a seat," one of the rougher-looking dudes said. We followed his instructions.

Sherri leaned closer to a skinny kid next to her, who looked more like a mongoose than a human. "Hey, sweetie," she said. "You got something for me?"

"Yeah, I got a dime," the mongoose replied.

She turned back to me. "Give me ten bucks."

I gave it to her. When the kid handed her something, she tossed it back and smiled. "Umm, good." She leaned back in the chair and waited.

It took a few minutes, but when it hit, she jumped up and started running around the room like she could fly.

"You want some?" the kid asked me.

"No," I replied. "I get all I want with marijuana."

"Aww crap," he said, rummaging through a bag of drugs. "All I have is smack."

"I don't use heroin," I told him, "but I have a friend who does. I might come back later and get some for his birthday." *Like with twenty police officers carrying automatic rifles.*

After observing these suspects for a few more minutes, I decided it was time to leave. "Come on, Sherri, let's go."

She didn't respond, instead dancing around as if she could float on air. It took about thirty minutes, but we finally wobbled downstairs. I had to hold her up all the way to the car, else she would have used the stairs as a runway and flown off to the stars.

During the drive back to the room, I thought how fortunate I was that she hadn't blown my cover. I definitely needed to watch my back around her, or I'd end up with a bullet in my frontside.

By the time she walked into my motel room, she could walk and talk... barely. I gave her the phone and told her to call a friend to come get her. Twenty minutes later, someone came and picked her up. I was glad to see her gone.

I waited two days before going back to the apartment. This time, I bought some marijuana and $100 of heroin. It was the black Mexican stuff, and very potent. I turned in my findings and the police went out and kicked the door open, taking everyone to jail, followed by prison. Scratch another drug-selling shop off the face of the earth.

I worked a few more assignments—mostly smaller towns—and didn't have much luck. The chief of police in Crane, Texas, brought me in to look for drugs, but after two months, I told him I was confident he had none in his city.

These undercover assignments were experiences I will never forget. Plus, working without backup kicked my adrenaline into a level I'll probably never feel again. Would I do these assignments today with no backup, and no one knowing that I was in town but the district attorney or lead detective? No. It's extremely dangerous and the drug money is too lucrative. Today, this money draws a much more sophisticated and vicious circle of dealers and distributors—all leading back to extremely deadly cartels. They don't mess around. Still, I worked undercover because my boss asked me. It was a job that had to get done.

While I was in Crane, Heather, my second daughter, was born. She was a beautiful baby and I was lucky to have her. With two healthy daughters, I was a very blessed man.

With the undercover assignments drying up, I went back on patrol. Late one night, we received a call from the FBI that there were three bank robbers in a motel at the west end of town. The Chief told us over the radio that he'd meet us out there, so we headed over to the motel.

Once everyone was in place, the FBI agents pointed out the room. Chief Banks led the way in his street clothes and house slippers. He wasn't even carrying a pistol.

I held a shotgun from the left side, and another patrolman aimed his shotgun from the right. Suddenly, Chief Banks kicked in the door and shouted, "Get down! Police! We are armed!"

We pointed our shotguns through the door and all three guys dropped to the floor. Today, there'd be multiple SWAT teams from different counties going in there, with each member wearing a helmet, face shield, and bulletproof vest. We had one bulletproof vest that was kept in my office in case it was ever needed. To outsiders, we may have looked like Deputy Barney Fife on *The Andy Griffith Show*. But even though we didn't wear vests and have all that high-tech equipment, we still managed to apprehend the bad guys without incident.

Two weeks after the motel raid, I received a call of a disturbance at a residence. Another patrolman and I responded, weaving through the city streets to get there. Because it was late at night, the streets were mostly empty.

We rolled up to this old house just in time see a large Hispanic man come out with a butcher knife at least ten inches long. As I got out of the patrol car, he stepped off the porch and began walking toward me. Something bad was about to happen; I just knew it.

As he came within fifteen feet, I jerked my pistol from the holster and pointed it at him, pulling back the hammer. Suddenly, he was ten feet away when I began squeezing the trigger. It wouldn't take much pressure to release the hammer, but then he stopped in his tracks and stared at me. I held my finger and waited to see what he would do.

Meanwhile, my partner was on the radio calling for backup. In no time, crusty old Sgt. Boyd showed up and produced a mean-looking shotgun. He calmly walked over to the man and put the gun up to his head, yelling at him to put the knife down or "I'll blow your head off!" It took three warnings, but he finally dropped it. It turned out he'd been drinking and was mad about something. Today, that man would be dead.

Back then, we always looked for ways to solve problems—ones that didn't involve death. We talked to people calmly. We backed up if need be so we could maintain a safe distance between us. I would have been justified in shooting that guy, but I didn't, and he's alive today. I have no idea if he did good or bad with his life. But I do know I let him live.

The demands on a police officer today are incredible. They are walking video recorders with an arsenal of weapons and body armor. They also have to know how to use nonlethal weapons like Mace, nightsticks, beanbag guns, and Tasers. I often wonder what would happen if the de-escalation techniques we used back then were mixed with the professional cop of today. Would we have fewer riots and police shootings? Or would we have more dead cops?

One of my fellow officers in Big Spring was Jesse Bedwell. He was a few years older than me, having joined the force when I was in high school. One day, Jesse was patrolling Interstate 20 when he noticed this big stocky black man walking down the side of the road. Jesse pulled over and got out of his patrol car, walking after the man to see if he needed help. Suddenly, the guy spun around and ran at Jesse, screaming, "I wanna see my mama! Wanna see my mama!"

The big man jumped on Jesse, taking him to the ground, punching and beating the heck out of him before Jesse could even come to grips with this new development. Instead of blocking his shots, Jesse took the blows so he could reach for his gun. As he jerked the gun free, he pointed it at the man to scare him, but he kept ranting and raving, hitting Jesse with everything he had. With no choice, Jesse fired into the man's chest. He fell over and died right there.

When I hired on to the police force, I told Jesse, "That man was going to kill you. You had no choice."

"Yeah," he said with a shaky voice. "It was either him or me."

During the investigation, he learned that the man was an escapee from the Rusk Mental Hospital in Rusk, Texas. He was truly mentally ill.

Thankfully, the ruling came down in favor of Jesse. He'd been justified, especially with the damage to his face. Even though there was no indictment, I knew he was shaken over it. Who wouldn't be?

We were friends outside of work, so I tried talking to him a few times to help with his anxiety. When we'd get off work, we'd stop and have some coffee. Sometimes we'd go practice our shooting. No matter what, I could see Jesse was suffering. And I knew he was drinking.

Day after day, that shooting continued to eat at him. Four years later, Jesse ended up drinking himself to death. That's when I learned a dead man could actually kill a cop.

It wasn't all doom and gloom. Sometimes we laughed.

One hot summer night, Jimmy Weldon Parks, a highway patrolman, came rushing into the police station in a panic. I happened to be there when he raced up to tell us this story.

"I stopped this vehicle on the frontage road of I-20 for expired tags. When I stepped out of the patrol car, I felt something squishy. It moved and started making rattling sounds. I felt something brush my leg and looked down to see a big fat rattlesnake. Since I had stepped on its body close to its head, it didn't have room to strike me. I danced around and crushed the rest of it. Man, that was close!"

Jimmy was shaken up, but we all had a good laugh. He was a big fellow and the thought of him dancing around on the road was hilarious. Yet he hadn't known what we did. On hot summer nights, the desert gets cold. To warm their blood, snakes often crawl onto the blacktop, which still hold the day's heat. What happened to him was actually common. Usually, though, the snakes slithered off when the car stopped. For some reason, his snake hadn't.

He got a lot of mileage out of that story, milking it for all it was worth. A few months later, he stopped a motorist on that same frontage road and got out of his patrol car, looking down for any snakes. That's when a drunk driver going the wrong way hit and killed Jimmy.

Sometimes a snake can be the least of your worries.

There was this real-life character named George McGann. He was born in Big Spring and had his dirty fingers in everything. George also had a temper, a real bad one. If he had a gun and something set him off, someone got killed. There was a story going around town that he was playing poker with some guys when a lady called and told him one of the players had been beating her up. He went in there and shot the guy dead. A real quality character.

George had a reputation as a hired killer for the Dixie Mafia. When someone needed killing, George was the man. He was also a robber. I guess if you don't mind killing people, robbing them isn't too big a leap.

Once, there was a poker game with a lot of cash. George busted in and robbed them. The next night, he showed up and bought chips to play. Everyone was so afraid they let him play. They didn't want to be rude by mentioning the previous night's robbery. At least he gave them a chance to win back their money.

George played a lot of poker and hit the high stakes games. He played with Doyle Brunson, Amarillo Slim, and a lot of big shots in West Texas. At the time, West Texas was the king of Texas Hold'em. There was a lot of oil money in play and sharp players knew the games to hit. Even though he had plenty of money for the big games, George was a lousy poker player. He needed another way to make a living, and robbing and killing filled the void.

I had seen George a lot, even stopped him for various traffic infractions. Each time he got out of the car, he was wearing a preacher's suit complemented by diamond pinkie rings and other fashionable accessories.

George was short, maybe five-two, and looked like an evil leprechaun from a Stephen King novel. If you were making a movie and he was in it, people would laugh and think he couldn't possibly have been real. But he was.

One night, I was on patrol when I heard over the radio that someone in Lubbock had killed George McGann. He was such a mythical character and so feared that it was huge news in our part of the country. It was like saying, "President Kennedy has been shot"—which, by the way, there was some rumor that George was involved in *that* assassination.

Anyway, the dispatcher said, "Public service me." That was code for, "Call the station on a landline. Stay off the radio." We knew some criminals had radios and listened in on our broadcasts. The last thing we wanted to do was send our strategy over the radio for them to hear.

I drove to a payphone and the desk sergeant picked up. "Listen, Roger, the killers of George McGann are headed to Big Spring right now. They're in a blue and white Cadillac." He gave me the license plate and I wrote it down. "Do you have all that?" he asked.

"Yes, I do. And you're not going to believe it, but I'm looking at the car right now. It's stopped at the light."

"Okay, let it go but follow it. Wait for backup. Understand?"

"Yes, I got it."

"Good, now go!"

I ran to the car and followed the killers. When the detectives pulled in behind me, they said in code over the radio to pull over the car. I did. The detectives came from behind me and arrested the men without incident. I heard someone went to jail, but was never sure they got the right guy. Still, everyone considered the elimination of George a real public service. Really, Hollywood should do a movie on this guy and cast George Clooney as me. I think it would be a huge hit.

One of the men who often talked to me about getting on the police force was Tiny Ellison. Tiny was huge—300 pounds—but gentle and caring. His real name was Jimmy Don Ellison. I'd known him from high school. When I went off to California and got married, he joined the Big Spring Police Department and learned the profession.

Once I got back from California, I frequented Herman's Restaurant, a popular hangout for the police on the main drag of Big Spring. They would meet there to have their morning coffee or midnight meal. I spent a lot of time there, hoping to find a way to get hired. By the time I did get a position, Tiny had moved over to the Howard County Sheriff's Office.

One night at two a.m., I was patrolling the streets with my partner. We were getting bored, so we went to the station to relieve the dispatcher. I had just sat down at the radio when Tiny called in. He was at his house and clocking out. I acknowledged this with a 10-4.

About an hour later, a sheriff's deputy called the station. I was still working the radio when he said, "Notify Sheriff Standard that Tiny Ellison is dead." The news shocked me. I'd just talked to Tiny. I couldn't believe it. How he died was even harder to believe.

According to the detective, Tiny was stepping out of his vehicle when he acknowledged to me that he was getting off for the night. As soon as he closed the car door, he was shot in the chest, throwing him to the ground. He was able to crawl on his hands and knees to his trailer, where his children stared out the window at his bleeding body. While they watched their father struggle, trying to crawl to safety, a man emerged from the bushes and stood over him with a gun to the back of his neck. Seconds passed until the gun blasted, ending Tiny's life just a few feet from his children. With his business complete, the gunman casually walked to his car and climbed in, driving off.

As this was relayed to us from the crime scene, I called Sheriff Standard at home and woke him up. As soon as he heard about Tiny, he hung up and headed to the scene. I told the desk sergeant I was staying on duty until they caught the killer—especially since I knew him. His name was Gilbert Martinez.

Martinez ran a bar called the Red Barn over on the north side of town. This was the same Red Barn that had been burglarized and I'd caught the juvenile inside about to stick me with a knife. I had worked for Martinez as a bouncer on Saturday nights, maintaining security when the crowd got too rowdy. I knew Martinez pretty well and couldn't see him being a coldblooded killer. I couldn't imagine what Tiny had done to him.

Within an hour, the town was flooded with lawmen. I, along with all our police officers, a posse of Texas Rangers, and every sheriff's deputy that existed, scoured the area looking for Martinez. Around seven in the morning, Sheriff Standard called to inform us that he and a Texas Ranger had found Martinez dead of a gunshot wound, sprawled on the floor of a little cabin he owned just north of Big Spring. Although Martinez was always kinda strange, I couldn't see him killing himself. I found it hard to believe that Martinez had decided to ambush Tiny and then slinked off into the woods to kill himself. The whole situation didn't feel right.

A full investigation was conducted, with every possible soul who knew Martinez and Ellison interviewed, including me. The final report read like a novel.

Apparently, Tiny's wife had been having an affair with Martinez and telling him how Tiny was whipping up on her. This lit up Martinez, who decided Tiny had to go. When Martinez died (however that happened), the case was closed. That left Tiny's wife free of both men and able to collect Tiny's death benefits and pay from the city, along with any life insurance they had. I don't think she lived in that trailer much longer.

The whole thing was very sad, because Tiny was a great guy and a solid patrolman. But it didn't make any difference. We buried him in a flag-draped coffin, and that was that.

CHAPTER NINE

On a hot night in early June, the summer was in full Texas swing. I was sitting at a table in the Stardust Club in Odessa drinking Coors beer, while Chief Banks nursed a whiskey and Coke just across from me. On either side of us were three more Big Spring police officers: Sgt. Don Thorpe, Sgt. Jack Boyd, and patrolman Ken Blackington. On stage was Willie Nelson. He was singing some of his hit songs as patrons danced below him. At the time, Willie Nelson was a good-looking fellow with short hair and could really sing. He was popular too; thus, the place was packed.

Sgt. Don Thorpe was also drinking beer, but with his right hand only because he'd recently been ambushed and shot in the left arm with a small-caliber handgun while checking out the bowling alley. Although I'd worked two nights and three days without sleep, we never found the shooter. Now, Don's left arm was in a sling—but at least it wasn't in a casket with the rest of him.

Sgt. Jack Boyd was next to the Chief, telling his war stories and drawing laughs from all of us. Ken Blackington, like me, was young, so we didn't say much. Recently, Ken had been with Officer Paul Alexander the night Paul had gotten his throat cut. He'd put Paul in the patrol car, driving him to the hospital. Paul would survive that attack but sport a nasty scar for the rest of his life. And years later, Ken would become a judge in Mesquite, Texas, a suburb of Dallas.

It was one of those nights when life was just right. The music was good, the drinks were cold, and the conversation fascinating. As the junior member of this group, I was enjoying myself, soaking up all the knowledge I could.

After a couple of rounds, we "convinced" Chief Banks to tell some more stories. First up was the case of the Big Boy Warrant.

"I was a deputy constable, just starting my career in law enforcement. Green as hell, but smart enough to know I could get killed doing this for a living." Chief Banks took another sip of his drink. "The constable handed me a warrant and told me to go serve it on this ol' boy in town. I knew his reputation, and he was real mean. The constable said, 'Now, watch out, Jay. Don't you get hurt.' I wasn't sure, but it was probably some kind of test.

"Well, I looked around and around until I finally found this ol' boy in a local bar. When I say 'this boy,' he was a really large man. And I ain't so small myself."

We chuckled as he patted his gut.

"So I walked into the bar and sat next to him. When he looked at me, I said very calmly, 'I need to talk to you outside.' He grinned and got up from the barstool, following me out. When we got outside, I told him I had a warrant for his arrest and had to take him in. Well, he looked down at me and said, 'What are *you* gonna do, little boy?' Then he just reared back and laughed good and hard.

"I stood there watching him laugh as I casually reached into my right-side pocket and slipped on some brass knuckles. I kind of chuckled too—smiling—so he thought I was afraid of him. Then, as fast as I could, I jerked my hand out and popped him on the side of the face. I was drawing my fist back to hit him again when his legs buckled and his brain decided to punch out for the night. All of a sudden, there I was, standing over Moby Dick.

"I dragged the guy to my car, huffing and puffing to get him in. The patrol car sagged to the right all the way to the station. I had three men come out and help me carry him to jail. While he was still knocked out, a doctor came and sewed up his jaw, wiring it shut."

He stopped, staring off for a moment, lost in the story. After taking another sip, he continued. "You know, I felt so sorry for that guy, that every day I went over to help him eat. I'd feed him with a spoon or a straw until he got well enough to get the braces and wires off. And you know what? We became friends after that and have been ever since."

He could see we all loved the story, so he kept going, especially when someone at another table sent over another round for us. He knew the man and waved at him before saying, "That fellow reminds me of Gene Paul Norris. Norris was a hired killer, bank robber, and burglar. He was a real piece of work. Usually, he worked out of Oklahoma, but sometimes he came down into North Texas. He always carried a long-barrel twelve-gauge shotgun. I was a Ranger and had him in jail on a murder charge. When it came time for trial, the witness didn't show up. I knew right then that Norris had gotten to him.

"As they announced that the witness was not present, I shoved my seat back and stood up loudly, walking over to the defense table where I faced his attorney and then Norris. As calmly as I could, I told Norris, 'You'd better go back to Oklahoma, because if you ever come back to Texas, I'm going to kill you.' I assumed that's exactly what Norris did. And good riddance.

"Six months later, one of my snitches called and said Norris was coming back to Dallas to rob the Fort Worth National Bank. I couldn't believe this guy. It was like he just wanted to piss all over me. The second I heard that, I called my buddy in Houston, Ranger Captain Johnny Klevenhagen. He had a murder warrant for Norris and set a speed record racing up to Fort Worth with his big ol' shotgun. We picked up the Tarrant County sheriff and an FBI agent and drove to the Fort Worth National Bank to stake it out. Johnny and I planned to sit there and watch for as long as it took. Unfortunately, Norris and his sidekick Humphrey spotted us.

"We took off after them and tried to force their car off the road, but Humphrey was a great driver with a fast car. In no time, we were racing all over the North Texas area. When we got close enough, the FBI agent and the sheriff stuck their guns out the window and blasted away, with Johnny's cannon going off at regular intervals. Humphrey eluded us while Norris stuck himself out and fired that twelve-gauge back at us. He was a good shot, popping our windshield and car with double-aught buckshot. I was swerving to make it hard for him to hit us, but that made it hard for *us* to hit *him*. We were lucky we didn't kill half of the population.

"As I gunned the car to over a hundred miles an hour, my passengers were terrified. The FBI agent yelled, 'Pull off! Pull off! It isn't worth it.' But Norris was too deep into me. Johnny too. No way I was slowing down. Yet I wasn't sure one of my passengers wouldn't jerk the wheel from me and wreck the car, so I kept an eye on both of them too.

"We were racing along when Norris turned onto a dirt road, speeding toward a river. Unless his car could fly or he knew a secret bridge that would allow just one car over, I figured we had him. Sure enough, he lost control and wrecked his car. As the car rolled over, Humphrey dropped out. But I was already on my feet and killed him right quick.

"I spotted Norris on the other side of the car, running toward the river. I gave chase with my little machine gun, which thankfully was fully loaded. As I caught up with him, I kept thinking about the number of men he had killed—at least fifty. I figured he was prepared to die like a man. But when I caught his leg with the first bullet, he tumbled in the dust, then the water, rolling around while still holding on to his shotgun. I ran closer, pumping more bullets into his worthless carcass, and I couldn't believe what I saw. He started crying.

"Now, that H&R Reising was a neat little submachine gun, but you had to get used to it. Its recoil pushes the next bullet an inch higher. So when I aimed at Norris's belly, I ended up stitching a straight line all the way up to his head. Twenty-one bullets they took out of him. But I'm telling you, gentlemen, I ain't seen nothing like it. He fell against the riverbank and tried to crawl out of the water, still alive. I ran down there and put the gun on semi-automatic, sticking the barrel right next to his ear. I pulled the trigger once and he didn't crawl anymore. It was like something out of a horror movie.

"When the rest of the police cars got there, I had to walk down to the riverbank and show them his body. I actually feared it wouldn't be there. But it was. I could even see the tears he had cried through the dust on his face. When they zipped up the body bag, I turned to the FBI agent and said, 'That's the end of Gene Paul Norris, the Smiling Killer.' It kind of put a smile on our faces."

At that moment and right on cue, Willie Nelson finished up a set and his band took a break. By now, we'd been drinking for some time. Ken and the two sergeants got up and went the restroom or to talk to some girls—or both. That left me alone with the Chief. Normally, I would've never probed into the Chief's past, but the beer urged me on. I decided to take a gamble.

"Chief, can I ask you a question? If you don't want to answer, I'll understand."

"Okay," he mumbled. "What is it?"

"Why did you leave the Texas Rangers?" At this time, he didn't know that I had read his letter of resignation—written to Homer Garrison, the director of the Texas Department of Safety. It was straight and to the point: "Since you have lost confidence in me, I submit my letter of resignation immediately," signed Capt. Jay Banks, Texas Rangers Dallas. Unfortunately, that wasn't much to go on for a curious lawman like me. I hoped my question would provide some clarity. It did.

"Roger, to become a captain in the Rangers, you have to stand out amongst the crowd. You also have to be well-liked by the men you're going to lead. This can be a double-edged sword. One edge gets you the rank, and the other edge chops your head off. As I was working my way up, I gained a lot of popularity with lawmen throughout the state. The governors I served under liked me. So did congressmen.

Even the state and federal officials liked me. In fact, most of the time anyone came to Dallas, they asked for me. One time, I even got to escort Miss Texas to New York City for a tour. I can't swear to it, but I felt Col. Garrison was getting jealous—maybe even thinking I wanted his job, which wasn't true. No way I wanted to sit behind a desk and run a big organization like that. I was happy right where I was, with lots of field work and action.

"Well, I was in Austin one time, and Col. Garrison called me into his office for a meeting. He stated clearly that he wanted the gambling houses shut down in Tarrant and Dallas counties. I told him it wasn't a good idea to close them, because the sheriffs of those counties got a lot of information from both the gamblers and employees. I said, 'Those gambling houses are like train stations. A lot of cases are made with the tips that pass through the mouths of the people there.'

"I reminded him of the time I'd gotten a tip from a gambler that Mickey Cohen was in Wichita Falls. Cohen had been a big-time gangster from Las Vegas looking to set up a mob-operated gambling house in the area. I'd gone straight to his hotel room in Wichita Falls, slapped him around some, and took his ass to the airport, putting him on the first flight to Las Vegas. So far, he's never come back. Of course, he's been in federal prison for a lot of years. But I told him if we closed these houses down, they'd go underground and we'd never get any information from them again. All we'd see was bodies floating down the Trinity River.

"I said my piece and Col. Garrison took it in. He said, 'Do you have anything else to say?' I said, 'No, sir,' and he dismissed me. On the way back to Dallas, I was pretty sure that he agreed with me and I could leave the houses open. I was dead certain I was right on this issue. Well, wouldn't you know it, about a month later, the Rangers came up from Austin and other parts and without my knowledge, raided the gambling houses in Fort Worth and Dallas. The sheriffs of Tarrant and Dallas counties called me up, raising hell. To them, I was double-crosser. At the very least, I was out of the loop and ineffective."

Chief Banks took in a deep breath and exhaled. "I thought hard about the news. Maybe Col. Garrison figured I was on the take and being paid to keep those gambling houses open. Or maybe he thought I'd gotten too big for my britches. Either way, I gave him the opening to get rid of me. My Texas Ranger career was over. The next morning, I submitted my resignation, and that's the way it was."

I nodded. His story matched up with what I'd heard. Plus, I'd seen clips in his office from his appearances on *The Tonight Show, Name That Tune,* and *What's My Line?* There was even a copy of his appearance in *Time* magazine. During his service, he'd been promoted as the perfect example of a Texas Ranger. With his size and sparkling image, the public ate it up. No wonder folks inside the organization couldn't wait to get rid of "that showboat."

I thought he was done talking, but I was wrong. Not by a long shot.

"Roger, I'm pretty sure I was set up. Col. Garrison and other Rangers knew I worked close with the local sheriffs and made a lot of cases from those gambling houses. I've learned that the people who set you up usually die a slow and painful death. For the folks who lie against you, that's their just reward from the great lawman in the sky.

"And guess what? Those gambling houses went underground and our information dried up. Period! It's like having a favorite fishing hole—one you know you can go to at any time and pull in some fish. One day, you go to your fishing hole and someone has filled it in with sand. It makes a man rightly mad."

"Well, at least the people of Big Spring love you," I said. "They'll never do that to you."

He laughed. "Roger, you're a young man, so you don't see the world as it really is. Let me tell you something. When I first came to Big Spring, crime was out of control. It's still too bad for my standards, but I had to get tough. And the first people I got tough with were the patrolmen. That's because cops love hanging out at the station. It's either warm or cool inside, depending on the season. And there's coffee and gossip. Also, it's the center of power. Cops love being near power, because maybe if they're seen, they'll get some of it. That's why I ordered my officers to spend more time out in the field. They patrol more hours. They spend more time writing up reports and gathering evidence instead of being back in the station pushing paper. And they don't like it one bit. But the public and criminals see them out there."

Straightening slightly, he leaned over the table and rested his elbows on its surface. "To me, that's a deterrence to the criminal and a comfort to the citizens. Plus, we get better reports and cases. But here's the deal. You start making enemies of the cops who want to hang out in the station waiting for a call, instead of in the car on the streets stopping crime before it happens. And each enemy you make, you're chalking up a mark—a person who goes around telling others how terrible and worthless you are. Eventually, these liars outnumber the truth and they can actually change reality—bend the truth so people believe you *are* terrible and worthless. Then they take your job and the crime wave starts all over again.

"Listen carefully, young Hammack, because I don't care who you are, whether you're the president of some big insurance company or the police chief of some tiny Texas town. You stay long enough, you make enemies. And when the number gets big enough, eventually, they'll come for you."

He let the moment linger before relaxing a little. "You have a good career ahead of you. If you keep doing good work, you'll be promoted. And trust me, one day they'll come for you. When they do, you'll need to make a decision. That's why I leave when I know my time is up. Power corrupts ordinary men. They want what you have: respect, a position. They want you to do their bidding. When you won't, they'll come for you. It's about control and power. You have it, and they want it. It's as simple as that."

We spotted the guys coming back, so the Chief leaned in across the table again, closer than before. "Listen, I'm proud of your work. The next opening for sergeant or detective is yours."

I smiled, imagining me as a detective. Unfortunately, Chief Banks knew what he was talking about. Even though he had been shot and survived seven gun battles, he wasn't able to fend off the politicians who wanted more power. They fired bullets he couldn't dodge. A few weeks after our night out in Odessa, Chief Banks was chased out of Big Spring, and twelve of us left with him.

I looked around and found a position working for Slim Gabrel in Odessa, Texas, about an hour southwest of Big Spring. He was the sheriff of Ector County. I packed up and moved my family, embracing the challenge of a new job in a new place.

I worked as a patrolman before being designated as a criminal investigator just two weeks into my new job. Before I started my new position, Sheriff Gabrel pulled me into his office and gave me some advice. "Roger, always see if the suspect will talk. Tell him you're interested in his side of the story. If you Mirandized them and they still talk, great. You might get lucky and get new information. If he doesn't, you'll be able to tell the jury at trial that you asked the defendant for his side of the story and he didn't give it. Sometimes he might give you evidence that shows he's innocent. An inexperienced or dirty cop won't ask the suspect for his side of the story. Yet a good detective cares about hearing both sides, and always confronts them with the evidence and see what they say. They probably won't have an answer, but who knows? They might. That's why the grand jury always wants to hear from the defendant. Do you understand?"

"Yes, sir," I said. "Either I lock him down as a liar and a criminal, or he gives me something that sets him free. That makes a lot of sense."

"Good, now get out there and do some crime fighting."

As I walked out of his office, I bumped into none other than Willie Nelson. I would see him often, because he was good friends with Sheriff Gabrel. How they knew each other, I had no idea.

After I started catching some cases, I decided to visit Chief Banks for some advice. We talked for a bit before I opened a fifth of whiskey I'd brought him as a gift and poured two drinks. I said, "It's been a great honor working for you, Chief. We'll get together another time, another place."

We clinked glasses and talked for a while, reminiscing about our adventures in Big Spring. As I was getting ready to leave, he looked around the room and got out of his chair. Opening his gun cabinet, he handed me his H&R Reising—the little submachine gun he'd used to kill Gene Paul Norris. "You keep this gun and be safe with it," he said, totally surprising me.

Stunned, I held it in my hands like it was a royal crown. His gesture meant so much to me that I left his house barely touching the ground. But, as I would later learn, Chief Banks and I still had a lot of adventures left in our bones.

CHAPTER TEN

Roger Hammack—Criminal Investigator for Ector County. It sounded nice. And it was.

As the new guy, I drew the night shift. One night, I received a call about an armed robbery at a gas station on Andrews Highway. I was the only investigator working that night, so I caught the case.

I went out there to find out what had happened. The case was somewhat unusual.

During the robbery, the clerk had been hit on the side of the head with a tire tool, breaking his jaw. He was in a lot of pain. Before the ambulance arrived, I was able to interview him and get his story, which wasn't much. He couldn't identify anybody or provide any details. He did say the robbers were a man and a woman. That narrowed it down to *everybody*.

I made a few notes, slapped the ambulance on the hindquarter, and sent it to the hospital. I went back to the office and let things go for the night.

Over the next couple days, I talked to a few people at the gas station. One informant came up to me and said, "Hey, this robbery was an inside job. That clerk—he was in on the robbery."

I was intrigued. Pulling the informant aside, I learned that the robber was female, in her twenties, and a heroin addict. I took all the information down and went back to my office to write up what I had. One of the captains came by and I called him over.

"I've got some information on this robbery out on Andrews Highway," I told him. "It seems that it was an inside job."

The captain said, "Naw, it couldn't be an inside job. That clerk got his jaw broke."

"Well, that's the information I've got. I'm gonna check it out and see what I can find."

A couple days later, I took the confession from the clerk and solved the whole case. I got a warrant for the female robber and went looking for her, but she had heard the winds of change were blowing and fled to Michigan. My nationwide warrant through NCIC nabbed her a week later.

I just happened to be walking down the hall and passed Chief Deputy Don Reeves and the captain who had previously told me that the robbery couldn't have been an inside job. Don Reeves turned to the captain and said, "Well, you were right. That robbery was an inside job. I never would have thought that."

The captain, seeing me there, turned red in the face. Evidently, he had taken my information and told people *he* was digging up tips and clues that pointed to an inside job. After listening to Chief Banks, I knew that you always run into people who will take credit for accomplishments they had no part in. Yet those same people will happily share blame with others when they themselves are at fault. I didn't see anything to be gained with arguing or debating the issue with these men—my superiors. I just walked away and let it go, never saying anything about it.

I grabbed my original warrant and went to Lansing, Michigan, picked up the female robber, and brought her down to Texas. We talked all the way back. She told me about other people who were dealing drugs in Ector County. I didn't take much of it seriously, because a drug addict will tell you just about anything. I figured that she was trying to get a reduced sentence.

Still, I took down all her information and went to the district attorney with it. He looked it over and knew some of the suspects. I told him, "If you could give her probation, she might help make some of these other guys. And really, she's not likely to succeed on probation. She'll end up right back in jail."

To my surprise, he agreed. The female robber was able to give us some information on some big-time drug dealers in Ector County, but the detectives couldn't get enough solid information to make any arrests. And just like I thought, she didn't last on probation and went to prison, where the clerk with the broken jaw already resided. He was supposed to get some of the cash, but he got the worst end of that deal. Hopefully, the blow-for-nothing caper knocked some sense into his head and straightened his life out, because I was pretty sure the female heroin addict was doomed.

During my time in Ector County, I worked a lot of interesting cases. One of them, though, stands head and shoulders above the rest. It was the case of Johnny Meadows. He was a brutal killer of women, racking up a body count that approached that of Gene Paul Norris. And he killed them in violent, sexual ways, leaving them in oil fields to lie in the sun where their bodies were almost mummified.

The case started with the disappearance of Gloria Sue Green, a secretary who lived in the area. Suspicion immediately fell on Meadows, who was suspected in many other murders. Of course, he left the area quickly and disappeared for a while. Before long, he popped up in New Mexico when authorities there arrested him on other charges. Sheriff Gabrel traveled to New Mexico to interview him in jail.

Through hard work, Gabrel got a confession from him. Gabrel told me later, "The guy has at least six different personalities. If you can bring the right one out, you can get some information."

I guess he finally got the right one out because Meadows told Sheriff Gabrel that Gloria was buried under a mattress out in an oil field. The sheriff called his deputies and they went out there and found poor Gloria, just a skeleton now.

I hired on when this predator was already in our jail. All of us in the station were ordered to stay away. The sheriff didn't want anyone to talk to Meadows but him.

One night, Sheriff Gabrel called me into his office and said, "Roger, I'm going to get Johnny Meadows out of his cell because I need to talk to him. Get your shotgun and bring it in. And put a shell in that chamber. If something happens and he gets loose, maybe even gets control of me, you shoot him even if you have to shoot through me. Just make damn sure that he never hits the street again."

He was dead serious, and I took him at his word.

Sheriff Gabrel took Meadows out of the cell without using handcuffs to let him feel comfortable and hopefully to get him talking. I swallowed hard when I first saw him. He looked like the devil. He had to be possessed with something. There was no doubt about it.

The jail was on the same floor as the criminal investigation division and my office. We passed by it as we escorted him into an empty office. I looked around and realized I was the only person there to stop Meadows from escaping. It was a big risk, one I'm sure the sheriff knew was needed to get him talking.

They closed the door and talked for hours. I could hear some mumbled words but was unable to make out anything coherent. I had to keep my distance in case Meadows emerged from the office and I had to shoot. I wanted some space so I had time to process the face I was about to splatter to kingdom come. I also didn't want his evil blood splattering on any part of me.

Sheriff Gabrel was a happy man, always smiling and saying hello to his employees. He usually shook my hand twice a day, as he did with the other employees. He was the opposite of the gruff and brooding Chief Banks. Yet both men were effective in their own way. That's why it was a relief to see his smiling face emerge from the office, ahead of Meadows. We walked the killer back to his cell without incident and exhaled loudly, thanking God it had gone smoothly.

As I unloaded my shotgun and put it away, I was pretty sure I wouldn't have shot the sheriff. But I also know I would've never let Meadows get out of the station. It would've been a tough choice.

A few months later, Meadows agreed to a change of venue in Dallas, where he'd plead guilty. Early one morning, I went up to get Meadows out of his jail cell. I had another deputy with me when I unlocked the door. There was also a reporter with us holding a camera.

I went into the cell and said, "Come on, Johnny. The sheriff is waiting for you."

Meadows got out of his bed and put his shirt on. I cuffed and escorted him downstairs. Per orders, I didn't use any leg irons. I escorted him to a vehicle and he got in with the sheriff. When the door slammed shut, they took off for Dallas and I was damn glad to be rid of him.

After he left us, it took a full month until his case appeared on the docket in Dallas. The district court brought Meadows out from his jail cell to accept his plea of guilty on four cases: Gloria Sue Green, Ruth Maynard, Linda Cougat, and Dorothy Smith. Meadows appeared calm before the judge and ready to enter his plea. As soon as the judge called his case, Meadows jumped out of his chair, yanked off his shirt, and yelled, "These people in the sheriff's office—the deputies—they branded me to get those confessions. Look, they burned me with irons to get me to say what they wanted."

Everyone was stunned, including the judge, because sure enough, he had four brands on his back—one each for Green, Cougat, Smith, and Maynard. They were perfect brands. When the judge finally recovered from this new development, he ordered the brands photographed and dismissed the cases based on the claim of torture and beating. They took Meadows back to his cell free of the charges while everyone scratched their heads. Thankfully, he had a hold from another jurisdiction, so he was staying in jail. This gave us time to investigate.

It didn't take long for the phone lines between Dallas and Odessa to burn up. The captain and chief deputy were discussing the situation when I happened to walk in and hear about it.

"You know, I'm the one who took him down to the sheriff's car," I told them. "I'm the one who got him out of his cell and I can remember this much: When I walked into his cell, he was lying on his belly and I saw nothing on his back."

"But Roger, he was wearing a T-shirt," the captain replied.

"No," I said, "he wasn't. Because I distinctly remember when he got out of bed, he put on a standard issue gray shirt—*not* a T-shirt. Plus, the news reporter was with me. They filmed me taking him down. I saw it on television that night."

The captain and chief deputy jumped on the phone and called the TV station, asking them to bring the film down to the police station. We all watched it, and sure enough Meadows didn't have a T-shirt on and his body was free of any marks and brands. Then, just like I remembered, he put on a gray jail shirt, leaving it unbuttoned and showing his belly. We all smiled because we knew we had him.

When we shipped the film and my statement to Dallas, they started investigating harder. It turned out Meadows was in a cell with a crafty inmate. They'd come up with this plan to use Blistex and a wire clothes hanger. The other inmate had used the hanger tip to scratch the skin and rub Blistex underneath the irritated skin. They did this over four days, because they had to keep getting more Blistex. Apparently, they knew that when Blistex was inserted into broken skin, it caused a blister. This made it look like a burning brand. Really, it was quite ingenious.

When this evidence was presented, Meadows finagled a plea on one case versus four and was sentenced to ninety-nine years in jail. I assumed he would die in jail, but with only one murder to your name, the parole board let him out after just eighteen years in prison. They felt he was rehabilitated and now a good citizen. Unfortunately, within twenty-four months of his release, he was headed back to prison for sexually assaulting a woman. I wondered how she felt about their decision.

Ten years later, this predator died in prison, taking with him a lot of unsolved murder cases. And that was the end of Johnny Meadows. (I heard he was inducted into the devil's hall of fame and wears an asbestos jacket to prove it.)

One of my jobs for Sheriff Gabrel was to run prisoners from our jail to the state prison in Huntsville. While there, I'd drop by Coryell County and visit with my family. My great-uncle Stony Hammack was one of those I loved talking to.

At the time, Stony was Justice of the Peace in Coryell County. He filled my mind with stories of our ancestors. On one occasion, we got to talking about the upcoming election. He said, "There's an old boy running for sheriff, but he doesn't have a chance because he's a foreigner."

"Where's he from?" I asked innocently.

"Oh, I don't know. East Texas or somewhere. But he's only been here about twenty years."

That story still rings in my head to this day. Later, I would know how right he was.

While I was working a case one evening, I happened to walk by the jail cell and see a little girl huddled up against the wall. This was a strange sight. We rarely had young kids in jail.

I nosed around and learned she was only twelve. Her name was Bonnie Perry and she had run away from home. They were holding her for the juvenile officers to talk to her the next morning. I watched Bonnie for a bit, then asked if anyone was coming to pick her up. She didn't know. "Maybe my daddy," was all she said.

When I looked at her, all I saw was a scared kid. Something inside caused me to feel sorry for her, because the next thing I knew, my lips were moving. "If no one comes to get you, get word to me and I'll take you home."

Sure enough, Bonnie told the county judge that Roger Hammack would take custody of her until she got things figured out. The judge, sure this was a big tale, called me in to confirm it. When I told him it was true, he shook his head and agreed, signing an order and giving me a copy.

That afternoon, I took Bonnie home to Mary. She drove the young girl to a shopping center and bought her some shoes and a new dress. Mary made Bonnie feel right at home.

A few days later, the judge gave me legal custody of her and made the daddy pay child support. I called the daddy and told him I didn't need his money, so he never paid.

When Slim Gabrel finished his term, a new sheriff took over—Elwood Hill. He was a great sheriff too. I stayed with him for a while until I got a call one day from Palestine, Texas.

"Roger, are you ready to put your crimefighting skills to work?" It was Chief Banks.

"Here in Odessa, I'm a criminal investigator working for a great guy in Sheriff Hill. That's a pretty good ante for the pot. You got any chips to raise with?"

He coughed into the phone. "As Chief of the Palestine Police Department, you'll be working with someone who can add to your crimefighting skills, maybe teach you a few more things. That's a pretty big raise."

I chuckled. "Well, you got me. I can't beat that. Let me give one week's notice and I'll be there next week."

"Hurry up," he said. "The crime here is getting worse by the day."

By now, Bonnie had been with us for over a year. I called her daddy to tell him we were moving to Palestine and were taking Bonnie with us if he didn't want her. He decided to come get her and Bonnie agreed. I called the county judge and told him I relinquished all custody of her. He said he'd sign an order and we said goodbye, with more than a few tears shed. She was a really great kid!

I arrived in Palestine, which is in East Texas, about halfway between Dallas and Houston. The size of my past two towns, based on the last census in 1970, was: Odessa—78,380 and Big Spring—28,735. To compare, Palestine was much smaller at 14,525. But for some reason, they had plenty of crime to go around.

It wasn't long before Chief Banks introduced me to Bobby Prince, a new Texas Ranger stationed in the area. Bobby Prince was a great big guy and easy to talk to. We got along great, meeting for lunch often.

One night, Bobby received some information that two guys were going to break into this building. He wanted to set up on it and see if he could catch them. I told him we could park my pickup with a camper there so he and a detective from our department could sit inside and watch. I offered to take the long way around the building and cover the rear since I was just a patrolman. He agreed.

That night, I made the quarter-mile hike and set up a position behind some bushes. All of a sudden, I heard Bobby Prince and the detective busting in the front door, so I pushed my way through the bushes just in time to see the burglars coming out the back. I pointed a gun at them and, to my surprise, they spun around and went back inside. The detective called for backup. Once we had enough men, we went in and made the arrest.

At the station, I visited with Bobby about the arrests while we filled in paperwork. We went over the entire night to see if we could improve on anything and do better. We agreed to meet for lunch next week and discuss it some more.

The afternoon of our lunch, Bobby told me his son, Randall Prince, had been shot by some punks with a BB gun. Randall was only five or six at the time. After lunch, Bobby and I decided to round up those punks and give them a good talking to. Once we produced some tears, we were hopeful the impact would last.

Bobby's son Randall grew up and became a Texas Ranger, just like his father. He has worked himself up the ladder and is now Lt. Colonel of DPS—second in command of the Texas Rangers. Not a bad way to honor his father.

It took several years, but the politicians in Palestine finally got Chief Banks. A bunch of us quit with him. He was disgusted with the politics of the job and told me, "If the politician owns a store, he wants round-the-clock police patrols to make sure no one breaks into it. But he's fine letting his competitor's store get burglarized. In fact, he may even wink and encourage it. Then the competitor is elected to the city council and he fires the worthless police chief who let his store get burglarized. The new chief comes in and guards his store and the whole cycle begins again. It's crazy and corrupt."

As I listened to him, I had another man whispering in my ear. It was Roland, my brother. "Come to Alaska," he said. "There's plenty of money up here."

"Alaska," I said to Mary. "Sounds exciting, yet dangerous. I'm thinking about giving this crimefighting a break and checking it out."

Mary said nothing because she knew me well. My mind was already made up.

"Alaska it is," I proclaimed, and began packing immediately.

CHAPTER ELEVEN

In 1969, my brother Roland finished his stint with the Navy. He had just gone through a divorce and was looking for a change of scenery, a new direction in his life. The economy was stagnant around Big Spring and Texas. This made it hard to find a job. He talked to our other brother Randy, who was also having employment challenges.

"Let's take a chance in Alaska," he told Randy. "A big pipeline is being built up there, all the way from North Alaska down to Valdez. I hear they're paying big money for working on it. What do you say?"

The pair talked about it and decided to go. Sure enough, they landed good jobs, making great money.

After the political execution of Chief Banks in Palestine, I was frustrated. I figured there had to be plenty of crime in Alaska. Surely, they'd need someone with my experience. The more I talked to my brothers, the more I liked what I heard. It sounded like an exciting opportunity.

In the spring of 1976, I said goodbye to Mary and the kids and boarded a plane to Alaska. After a long flight, I switched planes in Seattle and flew another four hours into Anchorage. And what a beautiful sight it was. The mountains were still covered with snow. Yet before me, the tall spruce trees spread out their green limbs in a wilderness panorama. After living in desert areas like Odessa and Big Spring for years, trees were a welcome luxury.

From Anchorage, I caught another flight to Kenai, where Randy waited for me. I stayed with him and his family for a week until

Roland came in from working on an oil platform at Cook Inlet. Both Roland and Randy showed me around. Things were indeed booming. Jobs and construction were everywhere. I just knew I could find a job in law enforcement, or at the very least as a security guard. I was wrong!

Each employee on the pipeline was a card-carrying member of a union. They'd already been union members when they came up from the lower forty-eight states. That included all the security guard jobs. And the local police didn't want outsiders. It was a very closed-off society.

With no options in law enforcement, I landed a job working in the oil field as a roustabout for Parker Drilling, a contractor that worked under Chevron. Roland was working for them too and got me on.

It was a good job, paying $10 an hour. That was the most I'd ever made. The job included an hour's drive each way. Still, I thought I'd get rich. Unfortunately, I could barely maintain a minimal standard of living. Since most goods had to be imported from the lower forty-eight, prices were exorbitant on everything. For example, white onions in Texas were ten cents a pound. In Alaska, they were ninety-nine cents a pound. Needless to say, we didn't waste one sliver of an onion—or anything else, for that matter.

Because my brothers had been here for the past seven years, they were solid Alaskans. Roland had an airplane—a two-seater Piper PA18 Super Cab. The Super Cab is probably the best bush plane ever built, almost impossible to overload. A good pilot could land it anywhere. During my first week, Roland flew me all over the area.

We skimmed over the mountains and glaciers, spotting goats and moose. Roland was such a good pilot he could get us within fifty feet of the goats on the side of the mountain. After he completed another two-week hitch on the oil platform, he declared it was time to go bear hunting.

We flew across Cook Inlet and made camp on a dry riverbed. The place reminded me of when we were kids camping out in the woods of Alabama and North Carolina, eating pork and beans. Maybe we were able to shoot a quail with our BB guns. I really enjoyed my time out there.

The next morning, we noticed a large black bear working its way down the mountain. We started walking toward it and got within four hundred yards. I decided to take a shot at it. When I hit the bear, it started rolling down the mountain. It took us about two hours to find him because he'd fallen behind some logs and was hard to see. I knew right then that Alaska was going to be the adventure of a lifetime. Little did I know I would stay there for twenty years.

During my time with Roland, he told me of an adventure he and Randy had experienced several years back. They'd been flying the Super Cab out on a hunting trip and found a spot to land. As he eased the plane down on the creek bed, they hit a log and wrecked the plane. After inspecting the plane, he found damage to the prop and fabric covering the frame. Another man flying a small plane saw the wreck, then spotted Roland and Randy waving. He landed to check on them.

The man flew Roland into Seward, Alaska, where Roland found a propeller and two rolls of 100 mph duct tape. The pilot graciously flew Roland back to his plane. He nodded his goodbyes, feeling like the two had the situation under control, and left.

Roland and Randy put the new prop on and used the duct tape to repair the fabric on the plane. Because the windshield was also broken, they taped it up so much there was only a small hole for Roland to see through. When they started the plane, the throttle was stuck wide open, threatening to ruin the engine. Roland quickly turned it off and regrouped.

"Listen," Roland told Randy, "this plane is going to be dangerous to fly with the throttle like this. I think it's best if I fly the plane home and send help for you."

Randy agreed. He helped Roland tie the plane to a tree to hold it in place until Roland gave the sign. Then Randy cut the rope with an axe and Roland took off in a slingshot maneuver. With the weather turning bad, Randy hunkered down in a tent and sleeping bag for warmth.

Randy was by himself for days, wondering if Roland had crashed or made it back safely. He managed to shoot a porcupine and eat it to stay alive. Sure enough, five long days later, a rescue plane arrived and brought Randy home. Welcome to Alaska.

After living on the lowest wages in Alaska, I finally landed a better job working on an oil rig—the same one Roland worked on. This was nice, because Roland and I now had the same days off. We worked two weeks and took one week off. It was a hard job, but it paid well—$1,000 each week. Getting a job that paid well helped convince me it was time to fly my family to Alaska.

In 1977, Mary and the kids flew to Alaska. Since there was a shortage of housing, we had to choose quickly and couldn't be too picky. And because the housing was so expensive, we rented a small three-bedroom house, grateful for that.

The area we chose was the Kenai Peninsula, a very beautiful place. Many times, we just walked or drove around the area sightseeing. Sometimes we'd go hiking. If we found a crystal-clear pool of water, little Heather and Regina would strip off their clothes and go swimming. Even in the summer—which averages fifty degrees—the water was very cold. Since I felt bad about being gone from my family for two long weeks, I was determined to spend as much time with my kids as I could. I wanted my family to live the good life.

While I worked steady on the rig, Mary and I were able to save money for the first time in our married life. And we were able to take good care of the kids. I really felt our family was on the right path.

In November, after several months of living together, Mary flew back to Texas and drove our vehicle to Seattle, Washington. There, she put it on a barge to Anchorage. Because this was our first winter in Alaska, we didn't know what to expect.

Up to this point, there had been very little snow. But by the time the car arrived, temperatures had dipped to minus forty degrees. Mary and I drove to Anchorage to pick it up at the dock. The car rolled off the covered barge and we drove it to the grocery store to do some shopping. I parked the car and locked the doors, thinking nothing about it.

Thirty minutes later, we came back and discovered the car door locks were frozen tight. I tried hard to get the doors open, but nothing worked. After standing out there freezing, I went back into the store and discovered that someone before me had found a way to profit from my misfortune. They'd created a methanol spray that melts ice instantly. When I applied it to the door locks, it worked perfectly.

I studied our groceries, which had been sitting on the pavement next to the car for thirty minutes. At forty below, they did all right.

With all the money I made, we splurged and bought some nice things: a four-wheel-drive pickup and a Piper PA-18 Super Cub airplane. During my week off, I could spend time with my family and then jump in the airplane and go hunting or fishing. Whatever the season, this was a great place to live.

When we first moved to Alaska, Heather was in kindergarten and Regina was in first grade. Children seem to be able to handle adventure better than adults. Even though it was so dramatically different from West Texas, it didn't take them long to adapt to Alaska. They were amazed at everything. When the salmon started running in the summer, both of my girls would catch their share of fish and help clean them. They didn't want to quit. They just wanted to keep on fishing.

We generally caught red salmon, since they were the best eating. However, we'd occasionally catch a pink salmon. We always released the pink ones so we could get our limit of red salmon, which was three each. These red salmon averaged twelve pounds each. With Mary, me, and Regina fishing, that brought in nine red salmon—at least one hundred pounds total, a pretty good stringer of fish.

We carried the salmon home. There, we cleaned and prepared them for the freezer. Once they were frozen, we were set for fish. Mary even canned some for the winter. Since most everything was imported and expensive, we saved a lot of money with fish, moose, and caribou. Like I said, it was a real adventure.

I could write a book about flying in Alaska, and maybe I will one day. But for now, these stories will have to do.

On one trip, Roland and I were flying through Lake Clark Pass and hit a blinding snowstorm, a real whiteout. That's when you can't tell up from down. Roland flew in circles while I watched for any signs of trees. Somehow, he flew the plane to the ground and made a perfect landing (one of the many times I knew we had God as our copilot).

The snow was very deep. We slept in our sleeping bags on the soft snow until it melted from my body warmth, turning it to ice and solid rock. The next morning, we packed down a runway with our snowshoes and made a successful takeoff for home.

Another time, I was moose hunting alone across Cook Inlet. Since it was November and twenty degrees below, there was already a lot of snow. I had to put skis on the plane. As I flew around, I spotted a large moose. Because it wasn't legal to fly and hunt on the same day, I circled around to land so I could make camp. I aimed for a flat piece of snow-covered land and made a perfect landing. However, when I stopped the plane, it broke through the ice.

I jumped out of the cockpit and saw the skis were two feet under water. I tried lifting a wing, but each time, I would break through the ice myself. I was lucky I had my hip boots on, because the water was ice cold.

I stopped and scratched my head, thinking about how to make this work. Then I found a log and tried to lift a ski, but the log also broke through the ice. I thought I was a goner. With no options left,

I climbed back into the plane and sat there, resting and praying for a miracle.

After a while, I decided to try the radio. Any other time, it would be impossible to transmit radio traffic while sitting on the ground. Still, I sent out a mayday call, changing the radio to several different frequencies. Incredibly, on my final distress call, a Northwest Airlines pilot on final approach to Anchorage Airport heard me. I was able to give him my location before he cut off. Thirty minutes later, a helicopter dropped out of the sky and snatched me up. It was a beautiful sight.

The next morning, I hired the same helicopter to help retrieve the plane. We hooked on to the frame and used the helicopter to move it 100 yards. This allowed me to take off and fly home. I couldn't afford to fly anymore that winter because it'd taken so much money to rescue the plane. I'm sure that moose had a good laugh.

My Alaskan adventures didn't always involve me getting out of jams. One time, we were the beautiful sight to another hunter. This one started when Alaska opened up some land to buyers for only the cost of surveying it. Roland and I staked off twenty acres, paying $1,500 for the survey. We built a cabin on the land because Roland and I were always together.

In March 1987, we decided to go check on the cabin and do some caribou hunting. We loaded up and headed out there, flying through Merrill Pass. To make this pass, a plane must be 4,500 feet above sea level. The highest point in the pass is a graveyard of planes that didn't make it. Fortunately, we made it through the pass and to the cabin.

The first thing you learn to do in Alaska is drain the oil from the plane's engine. You have to do this so you can heat it up with a Coleman stove and put it back in when you're ready to leave. That's how cold it gets.

When we woke up the next morning, it was twenty-five degrees below. Since we hadn't seen any caribou from the plane, we couldn't find a sign of them now. We made some coffee and heated the engine oil, deciding to fly somewhere else and look for caribou.

Once we were loaded up, the engine wouldn't start. Roland had to hand prop the plane—a dangerous maneuver. I sat in the pilot's seat to keep the engine going *if* he got it started. Sure enough, he did, and we were airborne fifteen minutes later.

As we flew around the vast wilderness, we noticed a cabin with smoke coming from the stovepipe. I asked Roland if he wanted to stop and check on it and he said sure. As I landed, a man came from the cabin and introduced himself as Pat Osborne. He was there alone, trapping. Pat stated he'd been dropped off about six weeks earlier and was almost out of food. He was desperate for some meat.

As we talked, I could tell Pat was a standoffish guy. This made sense, since he was out in the wilderness alone. I told him we had seen a herd of caribou at the foot of the hill and would circle them so he could see where they were. I also promised him if we made it back over here, I'd bring some food.

Roland took over flying and circled the caribou for Pat. Then we headed home, forgetting all about the man in the cabin.

A week later, I felt the strangest feeling but didn't know what it was. Try as I might, I couldn't shake this tingling. Something was wrong.

As I pondered what this meant, I wondered if we needed to go check on Pat. I went over to Roland's house and told him I wanted to go caribou hunting. He agreed and we decided to leave the next morning.

I told Mary about my strange feeling and asked her to pack extra supplies with plenty of food. I took a pair of bunny boots that are good for conditions like fifty below. Checking everything over, I tossed in a quart of coffee and a pair of coveralls. I never told Roland about my strange feeling, but I wanted him to fly the plane so I could watch for anything out of the ordinary.

My eyes were getting tired of looking when, out of nowhere, I saw a man standing on a frozen lake, waving his arms. It was Pat. I looked over to where his cabin had been and saw nothing but a pile of ashes. I showed Roland and he made a fast landing.

As we approached Pat, the first thing he said was that he'd been praying for us to come back for ten days. I nodded, because I knew God had sent us.

I handed him my huge thermos of coffee. As he drank the black coffee, I noticed he was completely black himself. I thought for sure frostbite had already set in. But he explained that it was soot from his old stove. He had fashioned it into a barrel that he could climb in and avoid the harsh winds while holding in his body heat. His crude invention saved his life.

I handed him all the winter gear we had so he could get warm. We stood by while he drank up the coffee and ate some food. When he was ready to go, we got him loaded up in the plane and took him home.

There, he climbed in the shower and stayed so long that it ran out of hot water. He was desperate to warm up. Once he was ready to talk, he told us his story.

A few days after we had left Pat and his cabin, his cookstove went out. He was putting fuel in it *inside* the cabin and spilled some. It caught fire and spread to the cotton curtains. In seconds, the ceiling was ablaze. In less than three minutes, his twelve-by-fifteen-foot cabin was engulfed, collapsing before him. It was 2:30 a.m. when he rushed outside wearing a pair of pants, socks, and a T-shirt. He reached back inside to grab a towel, but the heat was so intense it scorched his hair. With no food, shelter, and little clothing, he knew his life was over. Then he slapped himself to get a grip and survive.

He rigged up two fifty-five-gallon barrels for shelter, stitching the open sides together with wire to seal him inside. Using the leftover stove pipe from the destroyed cabin, he set it next to his campfire to transfer some heat for as long as it lasted—which wasn't long.

He breathed smoke and soot for ten days while praying for me and Roland to come back. The people who had dropped him off, despite agreeing to check on him periodically, had never once showed up. A frozen meal he had set out for the birds was all the food he had—hot dogs pecked by the birds with frozen rice. That was it! I was sure he wouldn't have made it a day more. He was almost gone, evidenced by the two weeks it took him to recover. Once he could move around, he thanked us profusely and left us for good.

A few days after Pat was gone, we saw a story with our photos on the front page of the local newspaper. And we were famous for fifteen long minutes. Then it was back to work.

There is a well-known saying in the oil patch: If you can't get it, you can't stay. I took that to heart when I landed a great-paying job with Parker Drilling. I knew my stuff and was confident I could handle most anything. Then, on December 20, 1987, I was put to the test.

I was working on a platform in Cook Inlet, deeply involved in the process of cementing the casing. The cementing program called for pumping a certain amount of water ahead of the cement. Because the mud in the well weighed 9.7 pounds per gallon against the water's 8.3 pounds per gallon, the water pushed an equal volume of mud back out.

Then trouble happened.

I was in the shaker room, a place where the heavy black mud first came out of the hole. There, *shakers* with screens separated the cuttings from the mud so the drilling mud could be reused. As I looked at the gauges, I noticed the mud levels were rising fast. This could mean only one thing: Gas had entered the well bore and was racing to the surface. We were headed for a deadly blowout. I had to act fast!

CHAPTER TWELVE

My body wanted to panic, but my police training kicked in and kept me in a state of calmness. I grabbed the microphone and called out that we were taking a kick and needed to shut in the well. This meant the Hydrill—the large diaphragms around the pipe—would close and stop the gas. It was a drastic measure, but one necessary to save lives.

I turned to the driller and yelled, "Shut it in!" Unfortunately, he had already reached the stairs and was running fast out of the command center. Even though we had been to specialized schools teaching us what to do in a blowout, none of us had yet to experience one firsthand. Each school had taught one clear concept: Get as far away from the rig as possible. Because we were on a rig out in the ocean, my first thought was to run to an escape capsule and be ready to abandon the platform. So that's what I did.

In front of and beside me were dozens of workers running for their lives. I'd reached the escape capsule when I was called back to the top of the platform. Stunned, I stopped and turned around.

Reaching the office, I was told that Houston control had called and wanted us to stay on the rig to pump mud down the hole. The idea was to kill the well.

This was crazy! It's like taking your helmet and covering a hand grenade before it explodes. Since we had time, it was much better to run and sort it out later. But then again, we wouldn't be taking the financial loss. All we had at stake was our lives.

By the time the driller and I got back to the floor, it was too late. Gas spewed out so fast it sounded like a freight train. The noise was unbearable. Still, we followed instructions and went to the mud room.

Grabbing some bags, we began mixing up heavy mud to shove down the well. In minutes, we were mixing and pumping the mud down as fast as we could.

We were told there was a boat coming, but not to rescue us. It was loaded with several more pallets of mud to mix. I couldn't believe it! Didn't they know gas was flammable?

Exhausted after thirty minutes of hard work, I took a break and walked over to get a cup of coffee from my thermos. That's when the place caught fire. The explosion was so loud it almost knocked me off my feet. As I ran across the top deck, I could feel the heat on my back. Somehow, we all made it to the escape capsule, lowering it to the water and floating away. As I looked back at the platform, the derrick just melted like an icicle, collapsing into a pile of molten steel.

Eventually, a rescue boat pulled us onboard. As I regained my composure, I could tell I wasn't right. A loud ringing in my ears made me unsteady on my feet. After we traveled the fifteen miles to shore, I called Mary. She had seen the news and was deathly afraid for me. She came immediately and picked me up.

Several days later, I went to see a doctor and he diagnosed me with severe vertigo due to damage to my eardrums. After two operations, which included a six-month recovery, I tried to put my life back together.

I soon learned of a medical block placed on my pilot's license. No more flying for me. Plus, I was physically unable to return to the oil industry. No more good-paying job. With all of that bad news, I knew I'd have to find a new profession to be able to stay in Alaska.

The first thing I did was sell my beloved Piper PA-18. This helped me make ends meet. Thank God that Mary's sister, Margaret

Sliger, was there to help us financially. And Roland would gladly fly me anywhere I wanted to go.

Falling back on my body shop work from high school, I was able to land a job as an insurance adjuster. Eventually, I was made a partner in the business. When Anchorage experienced an economic downturn, I found an office building being unloaded for cheap. I convinced three men—Gary Oathout, Neil Webster, and Law Henderson—to partner with me and buy it. We each put $2,500 down. Years later, when the economy rebounded, I did so well that one day I could afford to own two ranches in Texas!

We had been in Alaska for many years and not heard from our temporary daughter, Bonnie Perry—the one I'd brought home from jail. One day, she contacted me and wanted to come see us. We bought her a plane ticket and she arrived to the same amazement our two daughters had experienced. Bonnie stayed with us for three months before deciding to live in Anchorage. At the time, she was in her twenties.

Throughout the years, we received calls from her. She had a daughter and named her Heather, after our daughter. Later, she came down with throat cancer and had her voice box removed. So we started texting back and forth.

In July of 2018, I received a text message that she had moved to Wasilla, Alaska, and had some grandchildren. She said she still has great memories of us. And, of course, we loved having her. We were grateful to God we could help her.

But Bonnie wasn't the end of our childcare operation. After we were in Alaska for a few years, Mary received a phone call from her sister back in California. She was extremely distraught, telling Mary that her daughter-in-law had brought her two little boys over and dropped them off. The daughter-in-law said she didn't want her children anymore and just couldn't take care of them. Even though it sounds terribly cruel, we didn't judge her. After all, at least she admitted to that instead of doing something more drastic.

We knew Mary's sister was not in a position to handle two boys, so we decided to see if we could help. Mary and I put a pencil to it and figured we could provide a good home and stable environment for these little fellas. We put Mary on the next plane to California to check the scene out.

After a week, Mary arrived back in Alaska with two scared boys— five-year-old Robert and two-year-old Warren. They were so cute. We raised and loved them as our own.

It didn't take long to get the boys adapted to Alaska. After a few months rolled by, I told both boys that when they were eighteen, I'd adopt them if they wished. Robert passed on that offer. He got married and joined the Air Force, serving for four years. He's done real well for himself. He even earned a college degree. Now, he works for the Veterans Affairs and loves his job. We are so grateful he's a decent citizen. And we still feel like he's our son. We even call Robert's two girls, Meghan and Calista, our grandchildren. They know if they need something, they can always call Grandpa.

Warren, or Bino (a nickname he had when he arrived), was so young that he adjusted right away. In fact, Warren and I had more than one or two exciting adventures.

When I was still flying my Piper PA-18, he and I went hunting and fishing all over Alaska. On one occasion, Warren was seven and I took him 150 miles from home for caribou hunting. Since this was during the winter, the plane was equipped with skis.

After an hour and a half of flying, I noticed a herd of caribou. I circled them a few times, showing them to Warren. Then I landed on a frozen lake. We set up camp, which consisted of a tent, sleeping bags, and a small stove. Before long, the night temperature dropped to minus thirty degrees. I was worried, so I kept waking up to check on Warren during the night. He finally said he was okay and to quit waking him up. Somehow, I fell asleep.

The next morning, we woke up and looked out of the tent. There were caribou everywhere. Warren managed to load his rifle and we quietly crawled out of the tent. He found a perfect hiding place behind a little berm in the snow and took aim at a herd of ten caribou close to fifty yards in front of us. I told him to just pick out one and shoot it. With a 30/06 rifle, I explained the kick he would get when he pulled the trigger. He took his time and, sure enough, he pulled the trigger and a small caribou fell over. It was a good, clean shot. We quartered the caribou and packed it for the trip back. Then we took down the camp and I put the stove under the engine to heat up the thick oil. Even with this, the engine still wouldn't turn over.

With no choice, I had to hand crank the prop. This meant Warren would have to sit in the front seat and be ready to kill the engine if the plane took off. More than a few pilots have hand cranked their plane only to see it take off without them. Fortunately, Warren handled the task well and we managed to get the plane started and back home with no problems.

When he turned fourteen, Warren agreed to be adopted since his father had readily signed termination papers so he didn't have to pay child support. Today, Warren lives in California and works for the City of Modesto. He's doing great, especially with two of the sweetest little boys I've ever seen—Roger and Rowan. We love them to death. I hope he has fond memories of our adventures in Alaska.

Alaska is beautiful, but a very unforgiving place. A person must be prepared for anything, anytime. No matter what time of the year it is, a person should have a basic survival plan. In the summer, it rains a lot—and it's a *cold* rain. You need rain gear nearby at all times, along with some food and a weapon. Even if you're just going for a short walk on a hiking trail, carry a weapon (a handgun or at least pepper spray). The main reason for all this is one word: bears.

A mother and son were hiking just outside Anchorage when they were attacked by a female brown bear with cubs. They had nothing to protect themselves with and died right on the spot. Fish and Game decided not to hunt down and kill the bear because they'd been in the bear's territory.

While on a survey in the Swanson River Area, a crew walked past a bear's den and lost a man. I know this area very well, since I worked there for a year. I saw several bears roaming all around. Because of this, I am certain the survey crew saw the bear tracks that were always there. If they had been carrying a weapon, that man would still be alive. Again, Fish and Game let the bear go.

Another attack occurred in King Cove along the Alaska Peninsula, an area I also knew well. A six-year-old was walking with his family to the local garbage dump. They spotted a large brown bear and started running back to the village. Unfortunately, the bear caught the six-year-old boy and ate most of him before the village elders killed it. It was a tragic ending.

When they weighed the dark brown male, he topped 800 pounds. I have seen 1,000-pound bears. They are very strong. Their front legs are hard as rock. Now, I want you to think for a minute about raccoons. A raccoon might weigh ten pounds and most people wouldn't dare walk over and attempt to pick up a raccoon, or even corner one. A ten-pound raccoon could tear up a person. If you consider a large bear, imagine the damage he can do. It makes no sense to get anywhere near a bear, especially without protection.

Then there was the curious case of Timothy Treadwell. He lived out in the bear's environment making movies and generally trying to be with them. He had spent thirteen summers there and was getting close to leaving the Katmai National Park when two bears were spotted near his campsite foraging for fish and berries. It was late in the season, and both the salmon and berry production had prematurely thinned out. The bears were hungry, needing to put on more fat for the winter. This made them desperate.

Treadwell set up a camera to film them but left the cap on. The male bear must have heard him and turned to attack as evidenced by the audio captured on the film. Treadwell played dead and the bear left. But when his girlfriend emerged from the tent or he moved, the bear came back and ate him while he screamed. His girlfriend initially survived, but the bear caught and killed her, dragging the body to a hideaway to eat later.

Authorities found her journal entries and listened to the audio. This helped them locate the bear and kill it. When they sliced it open, they found most of Treadwell. Later, they located his girlfriend. And that was the end of the self-styled Grizzly Man.

My experiences were a lot safer. One time, Roland and I were flying and spotted a large brown bear at least ten feet tall. We buzzed the bear, causing him to stand up on his back legs like King Kong. As we came close, he lunged at us with his right front leg, desperately trying to grab our plane. We watched as he missed and crashed against a dead tree, knocking it over. Roland turned around and said, "He's clearing a spot for us to land."

Right!

Bears often check out areas where hunters leave their planes parked. It seems almost as if the bears are getting back at pilots for buzzing them. I've known several pilots who went out hunting and came back to find their plane demolished by a bear. That's the price of being out in bear country.

When Robert was about nine years old, I took him on a commercial fishing job with me one summer. We flew to King Salmon, refueled, and flew another two and a half hours where we hooked up with Roland. With time still left in the day, all three of us started setting out the gill nets, stretching them out about 600 feet from shore. This allowed the fish to swim into them and get hung up. We would pick out the best salmon and put them in a sixteen-foot boat. For a young boy, Robert was a lot of help.

We were there for about four weeks and caught a lot of fish. During this time, we stayed in a cabin right on the beach and saw large brown bears every day. Sometimes one would walk out into the water, lift up our net, and snatch a fish or two. We'd let him have his fill since we were in his territory and didn't want any problems with a thousand-pound bear, one that could knock our head off with just a slap.

Everyone in Alaska quickly learns about the many ways to die there. Freezing to death and bears are the most common. Unfortunately, Alaska claims more than its fair share of careless adventurers each year.

In 1972, President Nixon signed into law the Marine Mammal Protection Act. This law protects *all* marine mammals, including polar bears, from being hunted and killed for any purpose. However, Sen. Ted Stevens of Alaska put a provision in the bill allowing Alaskan natives to take any of the mammals for their livelihood.

I met Sen. Stevens one day in Kodiak, Alaska, and we talked for a while, becoming close friends. He told me he also put into the bill another provision that stated any marine mammal washing up on the beach could have its skull removed by anyone but nothing else could be taken. For example, if a person found a sea otter lying dead on the beach, the $10,000 hide would have to stay there and rot. Or if a person found a dead walrus on the beach, they could take the head and tusk but could not take the hide. The tusk would have to be taken to U.S. Fish and Wildlife and registered with them. The finder could never sell the tusk but could give it to family members who would then have to register it themselves.

The natives shot a lot of walrus, taking the meat to eat. Sometimes they'd shoot a walrus which escaped into the water and died. Later, it would wash up on the beach and rot. The only legal ivory in the world is beached walrus tusks. And Roland and I found several of them. We always registered them properly, with one of Roland's also scoring a three on the Boone and Crockett Club registry.

In the early eighties, Sen. Ted Kennedy came to Alaska with his boys and was taken around Walrus Island. This was a special island where the walrus spread out on the sand sunning themselves. (I'm sure this trip was paid for by the taxpayers.) We were not allowed to get close to this island and would have to fly at least 3,500 feet above it. Yet here was Sen. Kennedy and his boys close to the island and walrus.

One of the boys spotted a tusk lying in the water and was about to grab it. The wildlife officer told Sen. Kennedy that they couldn't keep it based on the Marine Mammal Act. It was reported to me that Sen. Kennedy told the officer he knew the law because he wrote it. When they landed in Anchorage, Fish and Wildlife officers were waiting to confiscate the tusk from Sen. Kennedy. I guess he should have read his own law before passing it.

In 1996, Mary and I decided it was time to go back to our roots. In other words, Texas!

At the time, the girls were grown and not living with us. We had only Warren. I went by myself to Midland to find and purchase a nice house. Then I waited for Mary and Warren to arrive, praying she'd love the house. She did. A week later, the furniture appeared, and we were set up.

We selected Midland because my mother lived there. I had purchased a home and car for her, wanting to keep an eye on her. However, I had the itch to move back to Coryell or Hamilton County. So I kept looking for a ranch in either county.

One day, I opened up the Midland paper and saw 220 acres for sale down by Fredericksburg. The price was fair—$125,000. I jumped in my car, went down there, and bought it. Just looking at the ranch, I knew I could make money off it. I closed and immediately began cleaning it up. Then I put a trailer house on it. I didn't know how to build a fence, so I hired a crew from San Angelo to fence it. I worked right alongside them and learned how to build a proper game fence. Once that was complete, I put exotic animals on the ranch. We'd lived there for four years when I put it back on the market, selling it for enough to pay cash for a place in Coryell County, which is where we really wanted to be.

Our new place was in Purmela, a town fifteen minutes to the west of Gatesville. With 285 acres, it was bigger than the last one. Like I did with the Fredericksburg ranch, I game-fenced it and set it up with exotic animals. Unlike the last fence job, I hired a helper and we fenced it together. And instead of putting a trailer on it, I built a nice house to complete the package.

Life was rolling right along when Roland decided it was time to leave Alaska. He wanted me to help him find a little ranch near mine. I looked and looked until I found the perfect place: a nice ranch right outside of Gatesville. Roland didn't have the money right then, so I made a deal with the seller that I would fence the spread within one year and pay him cash for the place, or he'd have a new fence all around his place and get to keep his ranch. He jumped on the offer.

Roland sold his airplane and came up with $50,000. I picked up the balance and we bought the place together. Excited, Roland began the long drive down from Alaska to his new ranch.

Exhausted from driving so many miles, he and his wife, Joy, stopped in Conrad, Montana, and went to sleep in a local motel. The next morning, Joy tried to wake him, but he was dead. When she called to tell me my best buddy was gone, I was devastated. It would take some time to get over this hurt. Then, my life would really change.

CHAPTER THIRTEEN

I t was a crushing blow.

After we buried Roland, I collected myself and realized I now owned two ranches. Since the Purmela ranch was in great shape, we sold it and moved to our new ranch in Gatesville.

By now, I was operating a nice business. It'd come about because of the fencing work I'd done on the Purmela ranch. When I bought that place, there was nothing there. I turned to my nephew, Israel Rodrigues, for help. He had a crew in Midland and brought them down to start framing the house. While he worked on that, I started building an eight-foot-tall perimeter game fence two and a half miles long. I had some exotics I needed to get moved onto the ranch, and I wanted the fence up when Israel finished the house. Yet game-fencing is not as simple as it looks.

The T-post is the main structural support of a fence. Getting that right is the key. The method I used was to drive each T-post in by hand. Unfortunately, I kept hitting rock. The only way around it was to hire someone to drill the post holes so I could come behind and cement the pipe in the hole. With just me doing the work, it was slow going. At the rate I was moving, the house would be finished long before the fence.

One day, I went to town for welding supplies. As I complained about my situation, I was told of a man who had the equipment to drive not only T-posts, but pipe as well. I contacted him and we talked for a while. He promised to be out the next morning.

Sure enough, he showed up and introduced himself as Bob Burns. Bob was a very nice man and we would become great friends until his death a few years later. He used a large air compressor that ran an air hammer and drill. The device would *drive* the T-post and pipe into the ground, right through rock. His crew made fast work of the supports, putting the pipe solidly in the ground. I let them handle it while I welded on the fence behind them.

During this time, Israel's housebuilding crew had gone back to Midland for a week to do some work there. When they returned, I was putting up the wire and finishing touches. They couldn't believe I'd gotten so much done. I told Israel my favorite saying from my oil patch days: If you can't get it, you can't stay. He laughed, then heartily agreed.

Other than Bob Burns, a neighbor, Jason Paul, stopped by occasionally to help me with the fence. This would be the second fence I'd ever built, and I loved every minute! I called our new place the Hammack Ranch.

A few weeks after the ranch was open, one of Bob's hands, Bill Barton, came by one evening and said he wanted to start his own fencing business. Ever since I had left Alaska, I'd felt guilty because I wasn't really contributing to society. I was fifty-five years old with some retirement coming in to support us. But I wanted to do something that would contribute to the county. I *needed* something to do.

After talking to Bill, I agreed to partner with him. I said, "Listen, I don't want a whole lot to do. Just a little bit of extra money to buy feed for my animals. Maybe we can do one or two jobs a month." Bill agreed, and we formed a fencing business.

The next day, I went out and bought all the equipment we needed. I told Bill, "I'll get the jobs, furnish all the equipment, and pay all the bills. You take care of running the fence jobs." We shook hands and got after it.

One call I made right away was to Bob. I told him I was starting my own fencing company with Bill, but would never bid against him on any job. Until his death, I never did.

Bill worked for a full month and said he didn't like being tied down. He wanted to do his little jobs and not be partners. That meant we had to break up the brand-new company. We did and remained good friends.

But with no partner to run the jobs, I had to reassess the situation. I had all this equipment and needed to put it to work. For me, there was only one option: I hired a couple hands and started building fences myself. I put up some advertisements, looking for one, maybe two jobs a month. Soon, though, I couldn't keep up. Today, I'm six months behind. This isn't bragging. We just do fencing so well that I quit advertising fifteen years ago.

"Let me stop you right there," my lawyer said. "Is any of this fencing stuff important to your case?"

"Yes," I told him. "It is. You'll see some of the characters involved early on and how they got tangled up in all this."

"Okay. I just don't want to get too far afield."

"Believe me, we aren't. It all ties together. You'll see."

"I'm getting hungry," he said. "Do you want to go out for lunch?"

"Mary is fixing up some sandwiches. She should be in here any minute. Is all this helping?" I asked.

"I think it is. But I need to see how this fencing business fits in with you being indicted."

"Don't worry, it's coming. You'll soon understand the connections."

"Okay, Roger. Let me grab a fresh pad and we can keep going."

The fencing company took off so well I could never find enough help. I probably hired a hundred people since I started building fences. Some would last a day or two, while others lasted years. Most of them would show only when they wanted to. But they all showed up on Friday—payday!

My philosophy is to hire anyone willing to work. Yet most prefer living off the system over working. I would talk to and encourage them to work more, try to get ahead in life. But if they made enough money to make it through the weekend, they were happy.

Part of the problem is that many of the folks I've hired have made some bad decisions in their lives. I feel everyone can use a second chance, and I want to be the one to give it to them. However, they do have to meet me halfway.

The other problem is that it's all outside work. Sometimes it gets pretty darn hot or freezing cold. A lot of workers like inside work where the wind doesn't blow and there's air conditioning. This job doesn't have that.

Try as I might, I just couldn't keep two crews together. I had to stay with one solid crew. Over the years, I had some good hands who took pride in what they were doing. I'm very proud of all of them, and hope they learned the trade well enough to start their own business.

One man working for me was Jonathan Hardy. He was quite the character. One day, we were building a fence right after a big rain. The fence line followed a flowing creek about six feet deep. Suddenly, I heard a large splash and saw Jonathan in the water. At first, I thought he'd fallen in the creek. Then I saw him come up with a snake in his hand. Looking closer, I could see the snake had a frog in his mouth. He grabbed the frog from the snake's mouth and let the snake go. As he crawled from the creek, he put the frog back on solid ground and wrung out his clothes.

"What the hell was that about?" I asked him.

"I don't know," he said. "I just heard the frog hollering, 'Help! Help! Help!' Next thing I know, I was rescuing him."

I wanted to get mad but couldn't. So I turned away and secretly smiled.

Another time, we were building a fence that required crossing a hundred-foot-wide creek. The water was six feet deep and no one wanted to cross it. As the leader, I walked over and began taking my pants off. Before I could get them past my knees, Jonathan had tied barbwire to the back of his belt and was swimming across the creek. He tied it off on the other side and swam back. As he got out of the creek, I told him with all the wire on him he would be rusted in the morning. He grinned and got back to work.

What I loved about fencing was the variety of jobs we took in. One of them dealt with a good friend named George Bynum. We had done a lot of work for George on his ranch in Purmela. His family went a long way back in Texas. As a matter of fact, his mother had worked for President Johnson.

George had a son named George Henry Bynum. This young man is a great person. However, he had a hard time with some reading skills. One day, I received a call from George. He told me he'd found a very good school for his son and he was doing great there. The school had mentioned to George it would be nice to have some fences built on the school property. They wanted to create a space where the students could go out and pet some animals. In other words, they wanted to create a petting zoo. George asked me if I'd be interested in building some fences for them. "You bet!" I said. "As soon as I get caught up I'll be right there."

About a month later, I took some of my crew to Weatherford, Texas, and started the job. I provided the materials and labor, and they paid me $1,500 for meals and motel rooms. I furnished the rest for free. I knew they didn't have the money because this work would've been a $5,000 job. It was a pleasure doing this for them. I knew it would benefit the kids greatly.

On the fourth weekend, we finished the job. Then we cleaned the fence line and drove off.

A few weeks later, I received an invitation to join the kids on a cookout at the school. My wife, Mary, and my nephew Bobby and his family went with me. We had a great time. Seeing the kids petting and playing with the animals made the whole thing worth it.

A few days later, the school sent us this note:

"We are so grateful to you and your team. Because of your hard work and kindness, we have a beautiful and safe place for our donkeys and goats. They spread love and joy into so many hearts. The kids who come here are hurting, and these sweet animals seem to take their troubles away. Our students often come to us feeling disconnected and anxious. After spending time with the animals, they leave connected and calm. Many of our students struggle with friendships, but here at the farm, they have Jenny, Annie, Gaya, and June, and learn that friendship takes many forms. We want to thank you for much more than the wonderful fencing. You and your team created a space for special animals with an important job to do. These four-legged teachers are helping heal the hearts of students with autism, trauma, and learning differences. Thank you for bringing our dream to life. In gratitude, Charlotte, John, and the kids of Springbox Farms."

It was the best thank-you I could get.

I received calls for fencing jobs all around Coryell County. One place I loved going to was Copperas Cove. The city has a special place in my family's heart and our history. Here's the story.

As the newcomers pushed out the Indians, civilization came in. An initial task of conquering this new world was surveying.

The purpose of surveying was to record the dimensions of the land—the height, width, and breadth. The surveyor would also note the land's features. Creeks, lakes, rivers, and springs were mandatory. People needed water. The survey would show its location.

Surveyors were a hardy bunch. They consisted of trained and educated men. They had to understand math. They had to be detail-oriented, and good at notetaking and map drawing. Yet they were marching into the wilderness, hacking makeshift trails through the forests and thickets. Many times, they were the first "Texan" to set foot on the land. Thus, they often discovered the new and hidden features of the land.

One such surveyor was Dan Hammack. He was my great-great-uncle. Uncle Dan was an educated backwoods man. He had been assigned to survey a mountainous area at the southern tip of Coryell County. It was a rugged place.

Long before the automobile appeared, the only way up these rocky protrusions was on foot and horseback. With no goods or services there, this made it mostly the province of Indians, rabbits, and coyotes. Uncle Dan would have to hack his way up and down it if he was to successfully complete the survey.

While deep into his survey, he and his crew came upon a spring at the foot of a mountain. They had been working hard, building up a great thirst. Uncle Dan, leading his men, decided to taste the spring and see if it was okay to drink.

Approaching the edge of the spring, he looked around for any wildlife or remaining Indians who might be happy to place an arrow into his chest. Seeing none, he dropped to one knee and reached into the clear spring. With his hand acting as a cup, he scooped out some water and tasted it.

"Egad, it's copperas," Uncle Dan said.

Copperas is believed to come from a medieval Latin phrase, *aqua cuprosa*. This means "copper water." Whether Uncle Dan knew Latin or not is debatable. Perhaps someone on the surveying crew did. Or maybe a scholar back at the office had made the notation. Regardless, after he uttered that phrase, the location was called Copperas Spring.

As time marched on and the railroad appeared, a need for a post office arose. Back in the day, far too many towns got their name from the post office. This particular location would be no different.

After the locals debated the potential names, two candidates emerged: The Cove and Copperas. Which one would win?

Another interesting feature that existed back in the day was something called "compromise." It's an animal rarely seen today. But in the 1800s, it was everywhere. People needed it to survive, to get things done.

After a great debate that surely involved long-winded speeches, fists pounded on barrel tops, and perhaps a drop or two of whiskey, a name for the post office was agreed to: Copperas Cove. And all thanks to a Hammack.*

I wonder what Uncle Dan would think.

We were building a fence one day east of Gatesville out in Flat, Texas. I was driving to the jobsite when I saw a vehicle pulled off the road and a man standing beside it. I made a U-turn and went back to help. There I found a man and three elderly women studying their flat tire.

I talked with the man and recognized him right away as Cotton Davidson. He was from Gatesville and played quarterback at Baylor University before being drafted by the Baltimore Colts. Later he played for the 1960s version of the Dallas Texans and Oakland Raiders. He was a big local football hero.

I told him to hang loose and I'd grab a crew member to change the flat for him. I went a mile down the road and got Vince Williams. We changed the tire pretty quick and he introduced himself as Cotton Davidson. I said, "Yeah, I know you." I introduced myself.

As we were getting ready to leave, he tried to give me five dollars and I wouldn't take it. Neither would Vince because he was on my payroll. We were happy to be of assistance. Yet now, thinking about it, I wished I would've had Cotton autograph that five-dollar bill and give it to me. Something like that had to be worth more than five bucks in Coryell County.

---

*Mears, Mildred Watkins. *Coryell County Scrapbook.* Texian Press, 1963, revised 1985. P. 78. Print.

Helping people was deep in my law enforcement roots. Recently, I took a call from the Cowboy Church out on West 84. They wanted a roping arena out there and had the pipe, but needed help. I sent my crew out and we drove all the pipe in the ground for them at no cost.

Opportunities to help people are everywhere. One evening, a lady in the Purmela area called me about her little grandson, who was handicapped. He had a dog that kept getting out on the street. This was very dangerous, because her boy would go on the street and try to get the dog back. She was worried about either her grandson or the dog getting run over.

Hearing this, we loaded up the truck and went out, building a fence around her house at no charge. After doing this for her, I received a call that would put me on the path to getting indicted.

In 2002, I went out to visit an elderly woman who lived south of Gatesville. She had a fence problem and needed some advice. She explained that she'd hired a crew to put up a chain-link fence around her house. This fence was needed to keep her dogs in the yard. I told her I'd check it out.

As I walked the length of the fence, I was sure this was a prank. In fact, I just knew I was on a TV show—one with hidden cameras where they trick unsuspecting people like me. I kept looking for the cameras and vans that were filming me, but I couldn't see any of them. They were well hidden.

Continuing with my inspection, I noted that the contractor—or TV director—had dug barely six inches into the ground, sticking the tip of the six-foot metal post down into a smattering of concrete, then stitched it together with chain-link fencing. With this shoddy construction, the entire fence line waved in the breeze. Really, if I just leaned against it, the fence would collapse.

I went to the gate and noticed an eight-inch gap there. Her large German shepherds had little trouble squeezing through. The more I talked with her and looked around, the more I realized this wasn't a prank or a hidden camera TV show. This poor old lady had been taken. It was very upsetting.

I explained that I would have to rebuild the entire fence. I would reuse the materials she already had, but the teardown and redo would cost $5,000. I suggested she immediately file a small claim against the contractor and I would testify about my fee. That way, she could get her money back from the contractor and pay me with those funds. She agreed.

On the day of the trial, I testified just like I'd promised. Judge Wood listened to the evidence, including my suggestion that we all go look at the fence. He said the court doesn't do that and he would make a ruling later. We left the courthouse hoping for justice.

A few days later, I found out he'd called someone else for a second opinion and they said the fence job would take only $1,500. That was how he ruled. Of course, the lady couldn't afford to pay me $5,000 with only $1,500 in funds, especially since she was out more than that when she'd paid for the fence the first time. As such, I left the whole mess alone. But it got me to thinking. *Is that how the civil laws really work? An old lady can be ripped off and it's just too bad?* I wondered what I could do about it.

Around this time, Mary was real sick—near death, actually. She had been on a waiting list for a liver transplant and living in Dallas for five months when a compatible one turned up just in time. It was a blessing from God, although I felt terrible for the family who donated it.

After the operation and three-month recovery, she was finally released from Baylor Hospital. I carefully and lovingly brought her to our ranch in Gatesville to see the completed house for the first time. She loved it!

Even though I couldn't get that fence rip-off job out of my mind, there wasn't much I could do about it. I needed to take care of my wife. But that would soon change.

As the months rolled by, my fencing business rocked right along. Mary got back to normal and was feeling great. This made me feel great too.

I spent my days driving through Coryell County, thinking back on my time in Big Spring and Palestine working for Chief Banks. I sure missed law enforcement. It had been almost twenty-five years since I'd strapped on a belt and pinned on a badge. And I sure missed being out there with people—helping them, enforcing the laws, catching thieves and burglars, and keeping the place safe for hard-working citizens. It was just something in my blood.

In 2003, while driving back to the ranch after a long day of building fences, I was listening to a local radio station and heard about the upcoming elections in Coryell County. The DJ mentioned how there didn't seem to be too much interest in the constable positions. With just a few days left, no one had signed up for Precinct 1. Since the county commissioner who represented me was in Precinct 1, I assumed I lived in Precinct 1 too.

I kicked it around for a few days, thinking back on my law enforcement experience and my long family history in helping establish Coryell County while serving as sheriffs and other elected positions. I thought, *You know, I might have a chance of getting elected constable.*

The next day was the absolute last chance to file for this position. I went down to Republican headquarters and talked to the chairperson, Judy Bernon. She was a very nice person and we became good friends, which is odd since my great-great-grandfather had been kicked out by the Republicans. Anyway, she urged me to sign up for the constable position of Precinct 1.

I went to the county clerk's office in the courthouse, where they directed me to a clerk. I had to fill out a bunch of paperwork and give them my address and I.D. When we were done, the county clerk came over and said, "I'm sorry, Mr. Hammock, but you can't run for that position because you don't live there. For constable, the road your ranch address is on means you actually live in Precinct 4."

I shook my head and went back to Republican Headquarters. When I told Judy, she said, "Well, you can run for that too. The constable there was appointed just a few months ago and is running on the Democratic ticket. Why don't you go ahead and run for Precinct 4? After all, that's where you live." So I signed up for the position, paid the fee, and started campaigning.

The primary was in March 2003, which I won because I had no opponent. My focus turned to the November general election.

I was determined to campaign as hard as possible. I took no campaign contributions. And I made every attempt to knock on each door in Precinct 4. To my surprise, Precinct 4 is the largest constable precinct in Coryell County, covering a lot of square miles. Before it was over, I was certain I'd visited ninety percent of the houses.

I met a lot of people and consider all of them my friends. Just like Will Rogers, who said he'd never met a person he didn't like, I'm the same way. When I meet someone, I consider them a friend until they prove otherwise.

Campaigning door-to-door was a lot of fun. I never knew who I'd meet. One afternoon, I went up and knocked on a door. Soon, a little old lady appeared.

"What can I do for you?" she asked, before inviting me inside.

"I'm Roger Hammack," I replied. "I'm running for constable."

She put a hand to her mouth. "My Lord, are you a Hammack?" When I told her I was, she said, "I knew your family. Many of them settled Coryell County. They were great people. I even knew your Uncle Warren." She went right down the line and named a bunch. Then she stopped and put her hands on her hips. "But honey, I'm a Democrat. I vote straight ticket."

Thinking like a politician, I quickly replied, "Well, sweetheart, you can vote for every Democrat on the ballot and vote for the only Republican you likely know."

She dropped her arms and smiled. "You know, I'll probably do that."

I gave her a big hug and told her that if she ever needed anything, to give me a call and I'd take care of it. I'm sad to say I never saw her again.

After months of campaigning, I learned that all the downtown people were already committed to my opponent, James Lee. They knew and liked him because he'd been a sheriff's deputy for a long time. There was no chance of getting their vote. That left the rural voters, so those were the ones I concentrated on.

Even though my family had been in Coryell since 1853, I was considered an outsider. The words of my great-uncle Stony Hammack rang true: "That old boy doesn't have a chance because he's a foreigner. He's only been here twenty years." I'd only been living in Coryell County for four years. That made me a complete stranger. Still, I worked hard and tried to meet everyone.

On election night, I went down to the Republican headquarters and waited. Once the returns started coming in, I learned I was ahead in the early voting. That was something to be happy about.

As the night wore on, my race pulled closer and closer. When it was all over, I won by twenty-five votes. I could hardly believe it. My opponent, James Lee, didn't want a recount. Instead, he went back to work for the sheriff's office as a deputy and stayed there until he retired.

Soon after, I got to know James real well. In fact, if I'd known him that well before the election, I wouldn't have ever run against him. He's a good man. He grew up in Gatesville and was a calf-roping rodeo star, winning several rodeos as a young man. I think he still ropes a little bit today.

Becoming constable made me swell with pride. I felt like my family history was coming alive in me. And I vowed to keep my promise: I'd be a good constable and help anyone who needed help.

A few days after I was elected, I spotted an old lady standing on the road waving me down. I had visited her house and remembered her sassy question, "Why should I vote for you?"

At the time, I'd told her the same thing I'd told everyone: "If you ever need anything, I'll be there for you." Now, as I pulled up alongside her, my selfish pride assumed she was going to congratulate me. I rolled down the window so I could accept her kind words.

"Howdy, ma'am," I said. "How are you doing today?"

She dispensed with the pleasantries. "Remember when you said you'd do anything for me if I needed you?"

"Yes," I said, still waiting for my congratulations.

"Well, the mailman forgot this letter. I need to get it in the mail. Can you turn around and take it to the post office?"

I blinked a few times at this change of course and collected myself. "Sure, no problem."

A few minutes later, I dropped the envelope in the box and smiled. *Well, Roger, I guess it's time to make good on that promise. Because if I can't get it, I can't stay!*

CHAPTER FOURTEEN

After the election, I had to wait almost two months to get sworn in. But finally, on January 1, 2004, at the age of fifty-eight, I took the oath of office and became constable of Precinct 4. I was so proud to represent the citizens I could hardly stand it. I just wanted to do the best job I could.

At the swearing-in ceremony, I was surrounded by a bunch of Democrats. To say I got the cold shoulder would be putting it mildly. For me, the atmosphere was downright frosty. That's why I went up to the only other Republicans present—the sheriff, Johnny Burks, and the county attorney, Brandon Belt—and told them how I looked forward to working with them. I also said I was very proud to be one of Coryell County's constables and would do whatever it took to be one of the best constables the county ever had. I'm sure behind my back there were more than a few eye rolls at this enthusiastic beaver.

Because the government was shut down for New Year's Day, I had to wait until January 2 to physically take office. It was a cold Friday when I went over to the justice building to check out my new workspace. To no surprise, I was greeted with little help or enthusiasm. I could understand their feelings. I had defeated a friend of theirs and was an unknown commodity. But I swore I'd treat them all with respect and trusted that when they got to know me, it would all work out.

Eventually, someone was kind enough to show me my office, and what I saw shocked me. Because the justice building had been a jail, my office was in the old jail kitchen. There was one desk with two chairs—one on each side. Foolishly, I thought the other chair was for any guest I might have. But no, it was for the constable of Precinct 3. We would share a desk and face each other.

I looked around and discovered there was no room to interview a witness or suspect about a crime or civil process. That was a problem. I plopped down in the nasty chair and just about fell backwards. I felt sure someone had switched it out before I'd gotten there.

I scanned the desk and could see I had very little area to work or write. But I soon learned why: Most of the constables did only what they absolutely had to do. Nothing more.

This was baffling to me, especially with the history and laws governing the office. In Texas, sheriffs and deputies have authority only within their county. Yet a Texas constable has all the authority of a sheriff and more. A constable's main job is to serve civil citations and warrants. To accomplish this, a constable's authority extends over the entire state. And Texas is a very big state—larger than California, and second only to Alaska.

A Texas constable also has the authority to wear his badge and weapon anywhere in the state, to help people wherever they are. Really, the range and depth of authority Texas grants a constable is amazing. That's why I was surprised that the constables either didn't understand their authority and responsibilities or didn't care. And frankly, I didn't take the time to learn which.

A necessary tool for a constable is an official patrol car. This is always furnished by the county. When they handed me the keys, I went to inspect it, thinking I might need to clean out the glove compartment. Instead, I stood there shaking my head. It was a complete piece of junk.

The small sedan had been handed down from the sheriff's office and obviously dumped on the constables. I could barely drive this rusted hunk of metal because the heater core leaked. Without a functioning heater, I had to drive with a frosted-over windshield—certainly a dangerous situation. If I'd been working for another police agency, I would've pulled someone over who couldn't see out their windshield. It was a head-on collision waiting to happen.

I checked the oil and it looked like red clay. With no other option, I hand-cranked all the windows down to clear the windshield, wrapped a jacket tight around my neck, and took the vehicle straight to the service station to have the oil and filter changed. As the patrol car coughed smoke along the way, the engine surged and stuttered. I could almost *feel* the gas draining out onto the streets of Coryell County, no doubt wasting taxpayers' money. What a shame.

As I sat in the service station waiting for the patrol car to be serviced, I pondered the situation. My fencing business was doing great. Plus, I had retirement coming in from my time in Alaska along with the money I'd made from selling the office building in Anchorage. Maybe I could put my money where my mouth was and use my personal vehicle? Sure, I'd have to pay for my own gas and the wear and tear on the vehicle, but it would definitely help me do my job. And wasn't that why the citizens of Coryell County had elected me? They didn't care how I got the job done, so long as I got it done. After all, if I couldn't get it, I couldn't stay.

I checked through the proper channels to ensure I could use my personal vehicle. They made it clear I would not be reimbursed for anything, and I told them I understood. Of course, my personal vehicle had to be modified with lights and decals. And that wouldn't be reimbursed either. But at least I could get to work performing the duties of my office.

I decided to drive the county vehicle on days where the temperature was higher so I wouldn't freeze with the windows down. As for the summer, I figured I'd deal with that when the heat came.

I went back to the office to pick up my county-issued gun and badge and discovered a second shock: I had to provide and pay for them out of my own pocket. Fortunately, I already had a good sidearm, but I still had to order a constable's badge. This was not a great beginning.

After that first day, I drove home thinking more about this new career. At that time, the pay for a constable was a mere $18,000. Most constables in Texas are retired deputies or sheriffs because they have separate funds coming in. Otherwise, they'd starve. If someone tried to make a living out of it, they were crazy—or corrupt. I laughed at the paltry amount and decided my $18,000 a year would cover the expenses of using my personal vehicle for official purposes. As for the leftover money, I'd use that to help Coryell County citizens wherever and whenever I could.

I awoke the next morning, a Saturday, and went to the feedstore to pick up a few things. To my surprise, I ran into Billy Jenkins—a fellow cop I'd worked with many years ago in Crane, Texas. This had been right before I'd headed off to Alaska. Billy congratulated me on becoming constable and shanghaied me to join him for a second breakfast. I couldn't turn down an old friend.

When the plates were cleared, we sat and enjoyed several cups of coffee. That's when Billy brought up our good buddy Sammy Long. Sammy worked for the DPS as a highway patrolman. He was a solid cop, too. When I'd been in Alaska a very short time, Sammy made a traffic stop on a cold November day. As he approached the vehicle, the driver stuck a gun out the window and fired, hitting Sammy in the right arm. Knocked to the ground, Sammy tried desperately to pull his weapon with his left hand as the driver jumped out and emptied his gun. Sammy continued struggling, his fingertips just pulling his gun out of its holster when the driver snatched Sammy's weapon and shot him in the back six times. Incredibly, a hunter was checking over his vehicle at a rest stop and saw the whole thing from 150 yards away. The hunter grabbed his rifle, took aim, and dropped the killer right next to Sammy. It was a trial, verdict, and execution all in one—Texas-style.

Billy told me that the killer had been some Navy serviceman who was AWOL. I guess he'd decided to murder someone rather than complete his service to his country—the same service he'd sworn to provide.

It was hard to swallow. Sammy had been a good cop with the DPS for eighteen years. He left his wife and son to carry on without him.

I asked Billy what Chief Banks would think about this, and he said, "The Chief would say losing good men is the unfortunate part of law enforcement. The public doesn't fully understand how dangerous it is to be a cop. But, on another point, the Chief would be completely shocked about the current state of law enforcement."

"What do you mean?" I asked.

"Back in the Chief's day—*our* day—we treated suspects and citizens with respect. But after killings like Sammy's, the police academies changed. Now, they teach control from the get-go. As soon as the cop opens the door of his patrol car, he's thinking control. He no longer asks. He orders. He demands. For most citizens, it's frightening. For some, it's offensive. This leads to all these violent body slams and beatings. The modern cop is pulling his gun quicker and the trigger more often.

"Law enforcement is no longer a de-escalation event. Instead, a monster emerges from the patrol car, hellbent on establishing control. This monster often escalates the situation—the exact opposite of what should happen and what we used to do. Deaths like Sammy's have been implanted into rookie cops by the academies, forcing them to think they're going to die during each stop. Now, unprecedented waves of citizens are dying. It's a crying shame."

I stared at Billy for a minute. This was quite profound. Yet I had no idea that at that very moment, what he was telling me would soon impact my life and threaten my freedom.

Billy went on to explain that when the escalation cops had started hitting the road, he decided to retire rather than change his ways. Now, he was grateful it wasn't him splashed across the nation's televisions. "You know all those videos of cops shooting citizens as they reach for a driver's license in their back pocket? Yep, I sure am glad it's not me."

I picked up the check, figuring his information was worth the price of the meal. When I shook his hand, he left me with this advice:

"You watch yourself, Roger. Your way of policing doesn't fit with these guys today. If you're not careful, they'll take you out too."

His words would be prophetic.

My first few months were quite an experience. I met my deskmate, Roger Huckabee, the constable of Precinct 3. He introduced himself and handed me a large stack of civil papers to be served. I couldn't believe the overwhelming backlog. Apparently, the previous constable had stopped serving them at some point. Constable Huckabee took the time to show me how to fill out the paperwork and enter the information in the log book, before returning a copy to court. I told him I appreciated his help and looked forward to working with him. Again, I wanted everyone to like me. If they couldn't, at least they might give me a chance.

As I leafed through the stacks of warrants, I noticed most of them were for insufficient checks. When someone hands a merchant a worthless check in exchange for goods or services, they're stealing. It's plain and simple. Sure, they may have made a mistake. We all do. But when the merchant calls or sends a letter and the checkwriter doesn't clear it up, it's stealing.

I spent hours at my tiny desk, sorting the warrants into piles. Through Chief Banks and other men in my life, I'd learned to work smarter *before* working harder. By arranging the warrants according to certain areas in the county, I could drive there and serve all of them at once. Of course, people don't make themselves easily available when the constable comes around. That's why I hoped to snag eighty percent on the first pass. I wasn't even close. It was more like twenty percent. Now they knew I was looking for them. This was going to be a long, hard grind.

After two months, the county notified me that I had used up my entire fuel budget for the year. "How is this possible?" the county judge asked. "No previous constable has ever spent this much on gas."

"Well, judge," I replied, "when I took office, I was handed a large stack of paperwork. I guess you need to ask the folks who didn't serve them or the folks who generated it. The good news is I'll be caught up in another month. Hopefully."

The county moved some money from the repair budget to cover the gas, which seemed to satisfy them for the moment. Still, I was pretty sure no one was going to make my job easy. If there was an obstacle that could be tossed in front of me, someone would make sure it happened.

By the end of March, I was completely caught up. I took a deep breath and decided it was time to address the crappy patrol car issue. I put the item on the agenda and went to speak to the county commissioners on the appointed day. When they called me up, I let them have it.

"The patrol car I drive was not fit for the sheriff's department. Why do you expect a constable to perform his duties in an unsafe vehicle and not the sheriff's department?"

"The sheriff's deputies drive their cars every day," a commissioner replied.

I was about to speak when they cut me off and moved to the next item. And that was the end of the patrol car issue. Thank God I had the personal funds to supplement the county's deficiencies.

Back at my office, I reviewed the next batch of warrants. Next to it was a large stack of pullover reports. In Texas, whenever a law enforcement officer stops someone for a traffic violation, a pullover report must be filled out. These are designed to monitor any racial profiling that might be going on. Because the paperwork was time-consuming and I was only a one-man office, I would have to be careful pulling people over for traffic violations. I had the authority to issue tickets, but really needed to save it for times I thought the person had a warrant. If I started pulling folks over too much, I'd be spending all my time filling out paperwork and in court instead of fulfilling my primary duties.

As I cleared up the backlog of insufficient check warrants, I developed a good routine. When I found the suspect, I arrested them but said I'd ask the judge to keep the fine low if they could make restitution to the vendors. It's the way warrants work that led me to this successful method.

Before, if someone wrote a worthless $40 check, they could plead guilty and get a $200 fine. If they chose, or if they were broke (the most likely scenario), they would sit the fine out in jail at the rate of $100 per day. Once they were released from jail, the only remedy to get the defendant to pay the $40 was a civil suit filed by the merchant. This required more money for court fees and myself, the process server. If the merchant won, they would spend more time and money trying to collect. Since the defendant was usually poor or a criminal, it was a losing proposition.

Using my method, I would get the judge to keep the fine very low—like $40—and transport the defendant back to the place of arrest so they wouldn't lose their job. But now, things were different. They knew if they still didn't pay, they'd be rearrested (more work for me) and put back in jail. Almost always, they wanted to avoid this yo-yo experience and found a way to pay the $80 plus court costs. This saved the county from housing an inmate for two days (a $120 expense), and the defendant was punished. The county served justice and made a little money on the fine and court costs, and the merchants got repaid. A win-win outcome.

One day, a man came up to me and introduced himself as Charles Ive. Charles told me his family had owned a Western Auto store in Gatesville many years earlier. He stated very clearly that if it hadn't been for Justice of the Peace Stony Hammack, his family would've been bankrupt. He said any time they received a bad check, Uncle Stony would always get it taken care of, often having the constable yank the criminal from bed and transport them to the jailhouse, where they would sit until someone brought him the money. Charles

Ive said he'd heard nothing but good things about me, as the money for unpaid goods was once again flowing back to the merchants.

"You're looking out for the merchants just like Stony Hammack," he said, clapping me on the back. "God bless you, Roger. Keep up the good work!"

I smiled as I left Charles and climbed into the county patrol vehicle. Noting the fuel tank was on empty, I went to fill it up, laughing at the county officials who would see another large gas bill coming through. I wondered if they wanted me to go back to the merchants and tell them the commissioners had cut my gas budget, so they would just have to write off their hot checks.

April was almost here, and I was looking forward to it. The warmer temperatures meant no more fogged-up windshields. One morning, I had just sat down at my desk when the phone rang. It was a lady in Temple, Texas.

"Constable Hammack," she said, "I hear you're someone who's willing to help people. Is that right?"

"Yes, ma'am. What can I do for you?"

"There's a warrant out on my son. He's back using drugs real bad." She started crying. "I love him so much, but I have to get him off the streets before he kills himself or someone else. I just couldn't live with myself if someone got hurt." She calmed down enough to explain that her son was driving around Gatesville in a black Ford Mustang. "Can you please help me?" she begged.

"I promise I'll do my best," I said as I picked up my notepad and jogged to my personally owned patrol vehicle.

I called the sheriff's office from my cell phone and talked to Deputy Dewey Wright. Together, we started looking for the young man on the streets of Gatesville.

Two days later, I cruised through one of the local motels and spotted the black Mustang. I contacted Deputy Wright for assistance and he arrived a few minutes later. After locating the suspect's room, I knocked on the door as Dewey stood ready to charge in. We could hear the man moving around, but he wouldn't open the door. Twenty-five years ago, we would have kicked in the door and arrested the suspect. But Dewey grabbed my arm and said, "You can't do that. We only have a misdemeanor warrant. We can't kick a door in for that."

There was no way we were going to leave without the suspect, so I called Judge Jimmy Woods to ask him how we could legally get inside. He said the only way was to have the motel owner unlock the door for us. "But Roger, you can't unlock it yourself."

With this information, I went to the office and told the clerk, "You need to come unlock this door for me so I can get this guy out on a warrant."

His jaw dropped. "Uhh, I ain't going to do that," he said, desperately looking for some paperwork to occupy himself.

I could tell he was scared. "Look, you come over there and I'll stand in front of you the whole time. Just unlock the door and push it open. If there's any shooting, I'll be the first one shot. Think of me as your own personal body armor." He rubbed his jaw nervously before deciding he just might survive.

I stood in front of the door as his nervous hand reached around me and unlocked it. When he pushed it open, the suspect was just lying there on the bed, half out of it. I explained the warrant for his arrest and handcuffed him. We searched the place and found some drugs, which we took into evidence. Then I called his mother.

"Ma'am, we got him," I told her.

"God bless you," she said. "I can't thank you enough."

Since the warrant was out of Temple, he would be transported there. His mother planned on visiting the jail and begging her son to go straight. But she assured me she wasn't going to bond him out or hire a lawyer. She made it clear he was on his own.

With the son safely locked up in jail, Dewey and I went back to the motel and examined the Mustang. The computer said the plates were registered to a Chevrolet, so we ran the Mustang's VIN number. It came back as a stolen vehicle. We had the car towed and it was eventually returned to its rightful owner.

On the way back to the justice building, Dewey said, "When we took down that motel room, I guess you planned on eating a round since you don't have a bulletproof vest. Right?"

"That's right. We never used them during my previous law enforcement career. They resembled life jackets—bulky and heavy. Instead, we just got shot and died."

"Well, Roger, things have changed. You might want to get one."

I made a mental note to check on that, although a bullet wasn't my biggest threat. Behind my back, groundwork was being laid for a different kind of bullet—one from my fellow officers.

CHAPTER FIFTEEN

Being a certified law enforcement officer is a key requirement for being a constable in Texas. Before the election, I called the Texas Commission on Law Enforcement and spoke to a clerk. I told her I had been to the Texas A&M Police Academy in the seventies and detailed my law enforcement experience. She said based on that, I could simply take the new test and be recertified once I passed it. The week after I was sworn in, I called the same clerk back and told her I was now officially a constable and needed to take the test. She promised to set everything up.

Days later, I received a distressing call. "Roger, I can't find any record that you ever attended the police academy, or that you have any prior law enforcement experience."

My heart began to race as panic bubbled in my chest. The current police academy was six months long. *And* it was full time. There was no way I could go to the academy and fulfill my duties for Coryell County.

I told the clerk I would check my records and see if I could find some evidence that might satisfy her. When I hung up the phone, I knew I was sunk. It had been thirty years. Chief Banks was dead. There was no way the archived records of Big Spring had any of my employment records. And when I thought about our move to Alaska and the sorting out we had done both going there and coming back, I knew I didn't have any thirty-year-old police academy records. After taking a few deep breaths, I set my mind to solving the problem.

First, I began researching police academies in Texas. I found one in Corsicana, an hour's drive from my ranch. It was held at their junior college at a cost of $2,000. I got all the information together and asked the county judge to let me talk to the commissioners at the next public meeting. When the day arrived, I told them what was happening and that I had located an academy to attend. I detailed the cost and asked the county to help with it. I also told them I'd be home every weekend to take care of any civil papers to be served. Even though Precinct 4 overlapped all the commissioners' precincts, each one of them voted no. Even the county judge voted no.

I told them that I'd pay for all of the expenses if they could authorize the sheriff's department to provide a deputy to periodically act as bailiff. Sheriff Johnny Burks told them he didn't have the manpower to do that. If it had been the other way around and I was sheriff, I would've told them that if I didn't have a deputy available, I'd handle it myself. The judge looked at me and said, "You should've known what you were getting into before you ran for constable."

"I knew what I was doing then, and I know what I'm doing now," I said. "I checked with the Texas Commission on Law Enforcement and they assured me all I had to do was take a test."

I noticed several smirks. They knew full well I had only 270 days to be reinstated or I'd have to resign my position. That would mean one less Republican. I gritted my teeth, determined not to let them win.

About three hours after the meeting, I was sitting at my desk when the phone rang. "Roger, I found it!" the clerk said. "You *did* attend the academy, so all you have to do is take the exam." I wanted to kiss her. She gave me a list of different towns that offered the test. I said nothing to the commissioners or county judge. Instead, I started studying the Penal Code, which was completely new from the time I was a cop. It was very complicated in some ways—especially the new drug laws, which listed chemical formulations. After poring through the drug schedules, I felt like a pharmacist.

I drove to the nearest town and took the test. I passed easily. After I received my reinstatement, I took the letter to the county judge and told him it was his responsibility to notify all the county commissioners at the next meeting. He stared at it for a while, as if completely stunned. I was sure some unlucky guy would receive a call shortly to hear that Roger Hammack had gotten his certification and the position he was going to be appointed to was no longer available. He'd just have to run against me in four years.

During this stressful time, I had spent many hours rummaging through boxes trying to find my old certification. I never did. But I did find an old photo of the H&R Reising submachine gun that Chief Jay Banks had given me. In 1995, years before I ran for constable, I realized Chief Bank's gun belonged in the Texas Ranger Museum. It was something I could and should do for my old friend and mentor.

I traveled to a Texas Ranger office in Midland because I had gone on raids with Capt. Jim Riddle in the 1970s. At that point, Capt. Riddle had passed away. But in his memory, I wanted that company of Texas Rangers to receive the gun. "And if you'd like to put it in the Waco museum, that would be nice," I said. "Or you can just keep it in Midland."

He agreed.

The next day, I went home and got the gun. The Ranger wanted to meet in the parking lot of the Midland headquarters, so I drove there. I watched as he put the gun in the trunk of his car. I didn't think I needed a receipt, so I didn't ask for one. It was the Texas Rangers, after all! They would take good care of it.

I never saw the gun again and hope that the Texas Rangers have enjoyed it as much as I did. It was a legendary gun owned by a legend.

When we moved onto Roland's ranch in Gatesville, I wanted to do something to honor him. In Alaska, he had set up a restaurant called It'll Do. I decided to name the ranch the same thing. So I ordered some metalwork and put the name over the entrance. I was satisfied and yet sad. I missed my brother every day.

Shortly after this event, my wife, Mary, was on Facebook and received a strange message. She showed it to me and I checked it out. What I discovered blew me away!

Early in Roland's life, he'd joined the Navy and found himself stationed in Scotland. During his time there, he'd met and married a local girl, bringing her back to Texas when his stint was over. Unfortunately, little Big Spring was too small for her. She loved big city living.

Roland tried hard to keep her there, but she went back to Scotland. Because she had relatives in New York City, he'd fly up there and meet her halfway. They spent a lot of time together in the Big Apple, trying to keep their marriage together. This went on for three years. Finally, they split for good and divorced.

When he met and married Joy, Roland still wanted to have kids. They never did. Then Roland died in that motel.

All this time, we knew Roland didn't have any kids. However, the Facebook message told a different story.

Putting on my detective's hat, I learned that Roland's first wife had gotten pregnant in New York City during one of their visits. Because they'd divorced shortly after, he'd never seen her pregnant. She kept it to herself and went back to Scotland with the baby.

I called the number in Scotland and had a hard time understanding the man on the other end. For sure, he wasn't speaking Texan. All I could really understand was that his name was Bobby and he was in his thirties. I invited Bobby to a reunion in July and he accepted.

On the day he arrived in Austin, Mary and I picked him up at the airport. Meeting face-to-face, I was staring at Roland. And we could more easily understand him.

We learned that his mother was still alive in Scotland. To date, she has never told Bobby why she kept his existence from Roland. That left us to try and fill in a part of life he didn't know. Lots of photos and stories were involved. So were barbeque and beer. Apparently, men from Scotland can handle both.

Bobby was thrilled to learn about his father. We accepted him as one of us, though we swore we weren't going to wear those kilts. By the time he left, he knew he was loved.

We invited Joy to meet her stepson, but she declined. After that, we didn't see or hear from her. For some reason, God gave us Bobby and took away Joy.

As the months rolled by, things settled down in the courthouse. I got along real well with two clerks, Linda Snively and Beverly Jones. Judge Jimmy Wood was also growing on me. That case in his court had been the main reason I'd run for constable. Now, working with him each week, I began to respect his wisdom. Even the Justice of the Peace Precinct 3, Larry McDonald became a good friend. Just like I'd hoped, we all worked together for the good of Coryell County.

On the job, I dressed the part. Even when I wasn't performing my official duties, I always wore my badge and weapon. As a law enforcement officer, you never know when a problem will pop up and need your attention. Too many off-duty officers are shot each year when they're mistaken for the perpetrator. It's sad, but true. Many times, I found myself working an accident, directing traffic, or dealing with a citizen who wanted to report a crime. Letting the public see me as a constable helped with whatever I was doing. And remember, a constable isn't just limited to that precinct. He or she has jurisdiction throughout the state. For the sake and protection of the citizens, it only made sense to always be prepared.

I kept the same attitude with my vehicle. Driving around, it had the proper lights and decals. And because the county refused to upgrade the patrol car, I drove my personal car a lot.

A good example of all this was an incident involving Carla Henderson in Flat, Texas. I had known Carla for several years. She was quite the woman. Carla had come to the United States from Holland still wearing wooden shoes. She was a hardworking woman, making a big success of herself in this great state.

One day, I was in town serving papers when Carla flagged me down. She told me someone had built a very ugly fence and attached it to her pretty fence. We talked for a while and I promised to drive over to her place and talk to the neighbor.

After taking care of my constable business, I went to her house and saw a man unloading cedar posts in his front yard. I went up to him, shook his hand, and introduced myself. We walked over to where he had attached his fence to Carla's fence and I explained the situation. Because he was a reasonable man, he could see how Carla might be upset. I told him I'd be glad to come out and assist him on standing his fence up since I had a fencing company. Since I was a constable, there wouldn't be any charge. Carla called me up the next day to say her neighbor had taken care of it.

Back in the day, this was how we policed. It was what I was used to. Friendliness, courtesy, and offers to help. An attitude like that goes a long way to solving most problems.

Another example of friendly yet professional policing happened one afternoon when a lady contacted me by phone and said her boyfriend had taken her vehicle without permission. She wanted my help in getting it back. I asked why she'd called me and this is the answer she gave: "I called the sheriff's office and they told me to write a letter to my boyfriend, giving him ten days to return the vehicle. Well, he doesn't open his mail and he's going to trash that car in two days. So one of my friends said to call Roger Hammack. He handles things like this."

I told her I wasn't sure why the sheriff's office had told her that, especially when someone had basically stolen her car. But I promised I'd look into it.

With the boyfriend's name, address, and telephone number, I did some research. Then I grabbed my paperwork and immediately went to his house. As I drove up, he was just pulling into his driveway. Before he was able to shut the gate, I was in his yard.

Startled, he came over. I introduced myself and shook his hand before asking him about the vehicle he was driving. He started offering up some excuse, watching me carefully as I took notes. When I showed him the vehicle's information regarding ownership on file with the state, he hesitated.

I stood there, listening and acting polite, yet feeling firm in my belief that he didn't have the proper authority to be driving that car. At some point, he cratered and asked, "Where do you want the vehicle?"

I told him he needed to get it to my office as soon as possible. He agreed. I said I'd follow him and give him a ride back. And that's what we did—except when we got to my office, he decided to walk back.

One hour after I had first talked with the woman, I called her with the good news. "Your car is parked outside my office and I have the keys. However, your boyfriend is walking back home. He may be lingering around, so wait at least thirty minutes before you come."

She waited a full hour. When she arrived, she was amazed. I walked her over to the sheriff's office so she could close her complaint with them. When she came back to my office, she told me she'd closed her complaint and told the deputies that Constable Roger Hammack had gotten her vehicle back and she didn't need their help. I was building up a lot of goodwill with Coryell citizens, but unfortunately, I was also making enemies in law enforcement.

Truancy was a big part of my job. Almost every day, the judge held court for kids who weren't going to school. Each day, for every child who shows up, the school receives a certain amount of money. This money comes from the state and is used to pay the teachers and maintain the facilities. When a student misses class, besides not learning, the school is docked money. That's why keeping kids in school is the mission of the school, the parents, and law enforcement.

The problem with all this is money. When the court fines the parents for their child missing school, they face economic hardships. Many of these children come from rough circumstances. They may not be properly clothed or fed. There may be drugs and alcohol in the household. God forbid, there may be violence.

One day, I was the bailiff for Judge Latham as he heard one truancy case after another. A twelve-year-old who was already on probation had landed on the docket again. Judge Latham heard the matter and fined her mother $50. There was no way they had the money. This meant her mother would have to leave the girl home alone while she sat out the fine in jail. After court, I approached the girl and her mother in the hall with a proposal: If the mother would deliver the girl to my house Saturday morning at nine, and the girl would help my wife with chores around the house, I'd pay her fine. She agreed, so I paid the fine right there.

Sure enough, the girl showed up on Saturday. I introduced her to Mary, who put the girl to work. I had fences to build so I left them alone. When I came in later that afternoon, Mary had taken the little girl home. "Well, how did it go?" I asked.

"We had a wonderful day! We put away the dishes and did a few other chores. Then we went to town, had our nails done, ate lunch, and went shopping for a couple of outfits. You know, the usual girl stuff."

The next Saturday, the girl called Mary, wanting to know if Mary had any other things for her to do. I would have let her come over, but Mary was out of town for the weekend. The good news with all this was that she never missed school again.

A few weeks later, I went to their house to check on the girl and found they had things pretty bad. I drove to a store and purchased a cook stove, hooking it up for them while Mary brought over a load of groceries. We continued checking in on them, buying some groceries and helping where we could. We also helped with their Christmas. I figured that's what my $18,000 constable salary was for.

Being poor is a bad spot to be in. As I said, my family came to Coryell County in 1853. Some did real well for themselves. They owned ranches, raised families, and lived out their lives as good, solid citizens. Others worked hard, but reached the end of their lives with nothing to show for it. They grew old and had no one to take care of them. For folks like that, there was only one place: the poor farm.

Poor farms were the earliest attempts at providing some social security. It was a safety net, although it was a ragged one.

A poor farm was often an abandoned or donated house that the county would fix up to make habitable. Homeless and poor people were then placed in the home and required to work for their keep. Everyone did what they were capable of. This included plowing fields, tending gardens, sewing, cooking, cleaning, milking cows—whatever was needed. Locals often donated some of their crop to keep the poor farm going. After all, seeing folks sleeping outside in the rain or freezing during winter was not the desired outcome of a civilized people.

In looking back through my family's history, we had several members who ended up dying on the poor farm. One of the reasons I ran for constable of Coryell County was to give back to the families who had taken care of the poor farm. In fact, my wife had been born on Poor Farm Road in Missouri. So I understand poverty. It's a desperate state to be in.

Throughout my life, my wife and I have tried to get people back on their feet. Many times, it has worked. Sometimes, we failed. I think that for those of us who have been blessed by the Lord, it's our duty to help people in need. Even the Bible mentions helping the poor, specifically by not going back through the fields twice and leaving the edges of the fields for the poor and widows to glean. That was truly the world's first social security plan.

I wish we had a world without poverty, without poor people. But perhaps we do because God wants to see how we respond. I hope He's been happy with my performance in that area. One day, I'm sure I'll find out.

As for the girl we helped, she's much older now. I still see her from time to time. She's doing good and has a bright future. Sometimes a kid just needs a little special attention.

There was another case, a boy. He was a senior in high school and facing a truancy charge. I learned from his father he was smoking a little marijuana. The father called me often about the boy. Each time he got out of hand, I'd go over and talk to him. I kept telling him, "You know, you have one choice in life. You can finish high school, or you can go to work for me on the fence line. If you can finish high school, you can make something of yourself. Whether you go to college or into the military, you'll have a chance if you'll just finish high school."

I don't know if that talk did anything, but we had no more problems with him in school. When he graduated high school, he joined the military. He advanced so much in the military that he's a specialist in getting rid of nerve gas. I shudder to think how you learn to do that. Needless to say, he's done great. I'm so proud of him.

These cases show the successes and challenges with truancy cases. Mary and I worked very close with a lot of parents. There were occasions where I'd go get a kid out of bed and take him to school. Or Mary would take them shopping to buy proper clothing, since that was a big reason some kids didn't go to school. We also helped out with rent money. Mary took diapers and formula to struggling mothers. On Saturdays, I had troubled boys out on my ranch working to cover the fine I'd paid for their parents. We helped as many kids as we could.

While we succeeded with some, we failed with others. As a constable and a human being, I did the best I could to determine which ones wanted help and which ones would respond in the right way. Sadly, what I was doing did not fit the mold of a modern-day elected official. Sure, I know there are examples of firemen and policemen who stop to help someone out of their own pocket. Yet in Coryell County, I was adding to the list of folks who didn't like me. One day, that list would grow fangs and bite back.

CHAPTER SIXTEEN

I was in my office sorting through the next stack of papers to be served when my good friend Deputy Dewey Wright appeared. He explained that his department had an order to seize some livestock. Apparently, the owner wasn't taking care of them.

I have a huge soft spot for animals. God put them on this earth for us to use and enjoy—not abuse and ignore. I get angry when I see someone neglecting their animals. If you can't take care of them, sell them to someone who can. Also, I have seen a common thread with people who neglect animals: They often neglect their children.

"Of course I'll help you," I said. "What do you need me to do?"

He explained that the sheriff's department had hired three cowboys with trailers to load up the animals. They were also taking ten trusties from the jail to help out. With those thirteen men and some other deputies, they felt they could handle everything. "What we need you to do is control traffic. There will be lots of trailers and vehicles parked on the street. As they're backing out and taking the animals to a holding pen in Gatesville, it's going to get confusing and dangerous."

Unlike the sheriff refusing to offer me help when it looked like I was going to have to attend the police academy, I readily agreed. I worked for the citizens of Coryell County. They didn't expect me to hold a grudge.

I arrived at the scene and it was as chaotic as I expected. I began directing traffic while they rounded up the animals. They were scattered everywhere, so this took longer than expected. After a while, another officer agreed to give me a break. I used this time to go to the bathroom. While I was on the property, I decided to walk around and check out the abuse. No telling when they might need another witness. That's when I bumped into the hand who had been hired by the owner to take care of these animals. He didn't seem fully capable of handling fifty horses, a cow, a pig, a calf, and twenty-five goats.

We made small talk for a bit when I asked about his background. He told me he had been injured in Iraq when his vehicle was blown up by a roadside bomb. All his buddies died. Only he survived, though he'd been found unconscious.

After being evacuated from the zone, he remained in a coma for four months. When he woke, he couldn't walk. Eventually, they sent him back to the states for rehab. Through two years of hard work, he learned to walk again. Still, I could see he was having a hard time with it.

He told me his sight was damaged too. All he had was twenty-five percent use of his eyes. With all this happening, the Army labeled him fully disabled and discharged him. This man, who had valiantly defended our country, was having a difficult time integrating back into society.

I told him how sorry I was, and to please contact me if he ever needed any help. We became friends. In fact, I consider most everybody I meet a friend—until they prove otherwise.

As we talked, I learned that the ranch was owned by a woman who had retired from the Army. She had fought in three wars for our country—Iraq twice and Afghanistan once. She had set up the ranch as a rescue for horses and other animals. None of this made sense.

I went and inspected the animals. First, I saw the cow. She was in bad shape, but I didn't get close enough to examine her teeth. It was possible the cow was at least twenty years old. She for sure wasn't giving milk.

When I inspected the horses, if anything they were *over*fed. To me, they were in good shape. I walked over to a large barn that was relatively new. Someone had spent some money on that. I looked for the goats, but they had been loaded up. Still, I said to myself, *There's something wrong here.*

Ten days later, I was the bailiff when the case came before Judge Coy Latham. The owner appeared and produced several receipts from the local veterinarian. She testified under oath that she had invested well over $200,000 in the buildings and other improvements. To me, that was credible. She also stated the goats were fed fairly often, but she'd wanted the brush cleared from the pasture where they were kept to make it easier for them to graze. She verified that she was a rescuer of horses, goats, chickens, ducks, and other animals. Some of the animals she took in were bad off because someone wasn't taking care of them. She said she'd spent all that money out of her own pocket. Nobody was donating or giving her money.

I listened and believed every word, especially since I had seen most of it myself. Then she called her veterinarian to the stand. He testified he had been out several times, treating the horses and other animals for a variety of ailments. He also swore under oath that he had never observed mistreatment or neglect. I began wondering how much investigation had actually been done.

More witnesses testified. One of the neighbors had filed a complaint, so the sheriff's department had gone out there and looked at the animals. They'd instructed the owner to fix a waterline. When the deputy went back out there, he found the waterline had not been fixed. With that, in addition to the neighbor who kept calling in and complaining, they convinced the county attorney to draw up a warrant to scize the animals.

Once the evidence was over, Judge Latham ruled that the horses would be returned to the defendant. To me, that was a no-brainer. Then he ruled that the cow, pig, and goats were in poor health and would be taken to the auction and sold, with the proceeds going to the county for their expenses. When court was over, the deputies and defendants wandered out to the lobby. I stayed with them to prevent any problems.

I was standing nearby when the disabled former soldier asked one of the deputies, "When are we going to get our horses back?"

The deputy said, "Hell, I don't know. But we damned sure ain't going to help you load them up. You need to find somebody to load them up for you."

I couldn't believe what I was hearing! The horses shouldn't have been seized, yet now these war vets would have to pay to get them back? And the sheriff's office had hired cowboys and used county trusties to load them. Why couldn't the sheriff get the trusties to help? After all, they were in jail.

The disabled vet looked over at me. "Roger, do you know anybody who can help us load these horses up?"

"Get the phone number of those cowboys," I said. "They'll help you, but you'll have to pay them. I'll send my brother Ronnie out there. I've got a thirty-two-foot trailer and he can haul as many loads as it takes. I won't charge you anything because it wouldn't be right, me being a constable. No way would I take advantage of a situation like this."

The deputies looked at me with malice. You could see the words on their lips. "Why would you help these people?" one of the deputies later told me. "You should've just stayed completely out of it."

"That's just the way I am," I told him.

At the time, I thought I was not only helping the war vets, but also the sheriff's office. Can anyone imagine a disabled vet and a single woman trying to load fifty horses? If either one had gotten hurt, the liability would have fallen on the county. To me, it was just good business to help people.

Two days later, when they had arranged to get the horses, I sent Ronnie and another ranch hand, Vince Williams. Vince was very strong. Together, they loaded and hauled three full trailers of horses back to the ranch. I instructed Ronnie and Vince not to accept any money from the owner. And sure enough, she tried to offer me money two or three times, but I wouldn't take it. I told her my constable's check took care of it. It was from this moment forward that my relationship with the sheriff's office deteriorated. I was sorry it fell apart, but if the same situation ever came up again, I would do the same—for anyone.

Because of this incident, the sheriff's deputies despised me. This I knew. What I didn't know was that the snowball had just started rolling down the mountain. Sure, it was small, but it would soon grow. Eventually, it would become an avalanche.

That derelict patrol car the county stuck me with punished me for years. Finally, they granted me mercy and replaced it. By this time, though, I was too used to driving my personal vehicle. Not only was it set up as an official vehicle, but it saved the county money on gas and maintenance. Another benefit of driving one of my personal vehicles was catching defendants off guard. Each day, I had to serve criminal warrants to people who didn't want to be found. It was a cat-and-mouse game. If I drove up in my patrol car and they saw me, they wouldn't answer the door. Sometimes they would flee. Since I couldn't kick in a door or drive through someone's backyard to catch them, they would get away. I had to be sneaky.

If the patrol car didn't work, I used my personal vehicle. If they recognized that, I used another one of my vehicles. This was the situation I was dealing with on a hot June day. A female defendant knew I was looking for her and was determined not to be caught. I'd been chasing her for two months. Finally, I caught a break.

Using my detective skills, I noticed her yard was freshly cut every Sunday. So, the next Sunday, I got in my personal vehicle and drove over to sit in her yard and catch her mowing it. Unfortunately, I was too late. I'd have to get there earlier next time.

When the next Sunday rolled around, I hopped in a gray Nissan pickup and took off. My crew had told me they'd hit a deer and damaged it. There was deer blood all over it, inside and out. I looked it over and didn't see much damage, even though it was extremely dirty.

One of the problems I've had with my crew is full disclosure. Sometimes they will damage a piece of equipment and not tell me. Only when we are about to use it will I discover it isn't working. This time, though, they'd told me about the deer and said the lights weren't working. Because I was driving in the daylight, I didn't need them. What they didn't tell me was the turn signals were also broken. They would let me find that out on my own.

Today, though, this old Nissan was my secret weapon. I knew the defendant had never seen me driving it because it was a crew truck. So I grabbed the paperwork and headed out early on Sunday morning.

My first stop was a car wash in town. I wanted to clean the truck up and make sure there wasn't any additional damage. After it was washed inside and out, I inspected the body and frame and found everything in order.

I hopped back in and headed to my sneaky defendant's house. It was time to serve an overdue warrant.

I came to a stop sign and spotted a city police officer watching the intersection. I signaled a turn and made it properly. Suddenly, I noticed the patrol car fall in behind me. He followed me for a bit before flipping on his lights. Seeing this, I immediately pulled over and killed the engine.

At this point, let me say that there is an unwritten rule not to write traffic citations to law enforcement officers when they are in the middle of performing their duties. None of us—city police, sheriff's deputies, or constables—make enough money to cover the risks that come with the job. For me, I couldn't even support myself on $18,000 a year, much less my family. The last thing any of us need is a $250 fine for doing our jobs. Also, many times, we are following a suspect or answering a call without our lights on. The element of surprise is sometimes vital. Of course, we don't want to abuse the privilege. The citizens just have to trust that a police officer is on official business when he rolls through a stop sign and not headed to the donut shop. I think the large majority of law enforcement officers don't abuse that privilege.

The second point I need to make is that my window was damaged and couldn't be rolled down. I'd known this when I'd gotten in the vehicle. Since that fact didn't affect its road-worthiness, I had no problem driving the pickup—especially since I had a warrant to serve. It would, however, affect my ability to interact with the Gatesville police officer getting out of his patrol car and walking toward me. That's why I opened the door and got out, showing him my empty hands, intent on identifying myself as Roger Hammack, Constable of Coryell County.

As we closed the distance, he started using the modern policing techniques of dominate and control. "Get back in the vehicle!" he ordered.

Knowing how this all worked, I didn't argue with him. That's how people get shot. Instead, I simply got back in the Nissan and closed the door.

Seconds later, he approached the window and saw that it was rolled up. This can be upsetting to an officer, because he wants a clear view of the cab as well as your hands. He also needs to see if you have a weapon nearby or perhaps contraband. A pane of glass can dull the scene or send reflections, which might give a criminal an edge. I knew all this. That's why I had exited the vehicle in the first place. I wanted to minimize the threat to the officer and the potential for a bullet in me. In the old days, we would have spoken to him when he got out, trying to learn why he didn't stay in the vehicle. The last thing you want is a person in a vehicle who you can't see clearly. But we weren't in the old days. We were in modern times, where citizens are body slammed and shot for reaching for their billfolds.

When the officer finally arrived at the window, he angrily knocked on it. "Roll the window down!"

I didn't blame him for getting mad. He was probably thinking I was some kind of smart ass.

"The window won't roll down," I said politely through the glass. "It's damaged."

"Open the door!" he demanded.

I could see he now understood why I had exited the vehicle. He could also see that if he had simply engaged me in a few words of conversation, we wouldn't be having this confrontation. Sadly, this poor officer's rocket had already ignited. Liftoff was seconds away. That's why I slowly opened the door and said nothing, letting him see my empty hands.

"I stopped you for no turn signal!" he barked.

In a calm voice, I offered the officer some relevant information. "I just took this car down to get it cleaned up. I was taking it to the shop in the morning. One of my crew members hit a deer with it and they told me they were having problems with the lights. I don't know if the turn signal works or not."

Ignoring all this, he asked, "You got your insurance papers?"

This was some more bad news. I had taken everything out of it because I had washed out the inside of the cab to remove the deer blood. "No," I said politely. "I just went down and cleaned it out. I took everything out of the car because I washed it inside and out. But if you run a twenty-eight on it, which is a registration check, it'll show you that I have insurance."

I want to tell the truth here. I was hoping he'd run a twenty-eight on it and see that I had the proper insurance. Unfortunately, when a rocket is lit, it burns up everything in its path. And I was about to be torched.

"Don't tell me how to do my job!" he snapped.

Obviously, he was inexperienced and scared. This was when the words of my good friend Billy Jenkins rattled around in my brain: "Law enforcement is no longer a de-escalation event. Instead, a monster emerges from the patrol car, hellbent on establishing control. This monster often escalates the situation—the exact opposite of what should happen and what we used to do."

I knew this and could see the officer had "lifted off." What I should have said was, "Yes, sir." Instead, like so many police videos we see on TV, the bullying and escalation began affecting me—pressing my buttons, getting me away from my professional demeanor. That's why I said, "Does the academy teach you boys how to be scared out here all the time with people?"

"Get out of the car!" he ordered. Now, it was on.

I got out of the car and he stood me at the rear, making me wait close to twenty minutes. While I stood there, I could tell he was punishing me. That's what all angry or inexperienced cops do. After being out there forever, I realized he was about to either harm me or set me up. That's why I slowly walked to my car to retrieve my cell phone. I wanted to call another law enforcement officer to stand by, so he could tell my wife how I was killed for an improper turn signal.

He darted out of the car and denied me access to my phone. Officers today know that a cell phone is a walking CSI unit. It can snap photos, record audio, shoot video, even copy documents. The last thing a cop wants you to do is use your cell phone to record his behavior. If they have to, they'll confiscate it from you and delete the damaging evidence. Of course, I'd never do that, because I wouldn't be doing what this officer was doing.

I asked the officer to get a supervisor out here, and that was one suggestion he thought had merit. I could tell he needed the help, and I certainly wanted another witness who would have to lie about how I died.

Soon, his sergeant arrived and we shook hands. I explained the entire situation to him and that I was trying to locate a person to serve civil papers. He knew me and knew I was a constable. I told him we could go together and see if the defendant was home. That way, he could verify I was on official business and not spinning some yarn to get out of a ticket.

The sergeant asked the officer what he was going to do.

"I'm going to write him a ticket!" he barked.

The sergeant frowned. "Well, okay. Roger, I guess you'll just have to see the city attorney about it."

I accepted the ticket and drove to the defendant's house, finding her yard cut minutes earlier. I had missed her again. It would take another month and more gas in the patrol car charged to the county to finally get her.

I went home and sat at my desk, staring at the ticket. The sergeant had told me to see the county attorney. It was Tommy Haggerty. When I said that name out loud, I knew this problem would get worse. I had history with him and it wasn't good. Really, the last person I needed to visit with was Tommy Haggerty. My life was going to get worse before it got better.

CHAPTER SEVENTEEN

I thought about Tommy Haggerty on the way home. Our last encounter didn't go well. It all had to do with Shorty.

Years earlier, a woman had come into the justice of the peace's office and talked with Judge Wood about a problem she was having with her husband. When she left, Judge Wood called me into his office. "Roger, would you talk to this woman's husband about treating her badly?"

He handed me the information and I looked it over. "Judge, I know this fella."

"Well, then, maybe you can talk some sense into him."

I left the courthouse and drove by the man's house. He happened to be out front, so I pulled up and had a nice talk with him. After that, he never bothered the woman again.

Later that day, I happened to see that same woman and asked if she needed a job.

"Yes, sir," she said politely. "I could sure use some income."

She said her nickname was Shorty, mainly because she was four feet, six inches tall. I didn't expect much out of her, but that wasn't the point. She needed help and I could provide it.

The first day I put her on a fence line, I had to make sure of what I was seeing. She was outworking every man I'd ever hired, including me. In fastening the barbwire to the T-posts, she was out-clipping us two to one. And she kept it up all day long. The next day, I expected she would slow down, but she didn't. That was her normal pace.

Each day, all week long for months on end, Shorty outworked my entire crew, saving me her salary.

When we took breaks, I noticed she sat off by herself, not socializing with any of us. That was okay with me. She'd had a rough time with men and probably didn't want to be around them any longer than necessary.

After going on like this for a while, we found ourselves alone one day, waiting on a delivery of materials. I casually broached the subject of her past and she told me about it. She did admit to having serious problems going all the way back to childhood. It was definitely raw. Now, her mom had custody of her kids and wouldn't let her see them. Shorty said she'd gotten herself together. "If only I could see them," she said with a sad sigh. "What a difference that would make."

I probed her more and discovered she had a court order to see the kids, who lived in neighboring Hamilton County. After I'd read it, Shorty and I drove to Hamilton County and stopped in to talk with the newly elected sheriff there—Gregg Bewley. I knew Gregg from when he'd been a deputy in Coryell County. I showed him the court order and explained that I would go as a peace officer and do the civil standby myself so she could see her kids. Sheriff Bewley was fine with me doing that.

We drove to the house and the situation turned into a problem in less than a minute. Shorty and her mom screamed and hollered at each other. Despite a court order and facing certain jail time, her mother absolutely would not let Shorty see the kids. I got on the phone and called the sheriff's department, requesting backup. They arrived pretty quickly and I explained what had happened. After some discussion back and forth, I made the call to take Shorty and leave. We drove back to Gatesville and I dropped her off at her apartment.

At home, I got to thinking about what had just happened. I was in another county, even though I was a constable who could serve warrants and papers in adjoining counties. I got worried about whether I would face civil liability, because a lot of constables get sued over civil standbys. I didn't want the county being sued over this. So I went to the Coryell County Attorney Brandon Belt and detailed what had happened. He looked at Shorty's papers and said, "No, you weren't on official duty over there. You weren't serving papers. If they sued, you'd be sued personally, not the county."

That wasn't great, but at least the taxpayers wouldn't have to pay for me helping someone. I knew as constable, I could perform my official duties anywhere in the state of Texas. However, I now knew that according to Brandon's advice, I was off duty and on my own if I was in Hamilton County and not serving papers.

A few days later, Shorty and I talked about this sad state of affairs. "Why don't you get an attorney and see what you can do?" I asked Shorty.

"Yeah, I've been thinking about that. I want to hire attorney Tommy Haggerty, but I don't have enough money saved up yet."

"How much do you need?" I asked.

"Twenty-five hundred dollars."

As hard as Shorty worked, she was a bargain. "I'll front you the twenty-five hundred and take a little from your wages each week. You go hire that lawyer and start seeing your kids."

Two months later, I got to talking to Shorty about her court case. I listened as she explained how her attorney always agreed with the other attorney and wasn't doing his job. Shorty gave me some examples and I grew concerned. She was scheduled to meet with her attorney in a few days and agreed to let me come along.

During the meeting, everything was discussed. After seeing and hearing what was going on, I told Tommy Haggerty, "You're getting out-lawyered at every corner!"

Tommy blew up at me. "If you want to get another attorney, you go ahead and get another attorney!" At this point, he was a private practice lawyer and not yet the city attorney.

I told Shorty, "Just fire that guy. I know another attorney around the corner from here. I've seen him operate in court. We'll hire him."

So we went to see the other attorney. When I told him about the situation, he refused to take any money. He was one of these guys who knew helping people was never the wrong thing to do. He read over the file and wrote one letter to Shorty's mother's attorney and it was settled.

One letter!

Suddenly, Shorty was able to visit her kids. Today, her kids are grown and getting along fine with their mother—no thanks to Tommy Haggerty.

I thought about my ticket situation again. Tommy was now the Gatesville's City Attorney. No way he was going to dismiss that ticket, not after Shorty's child custody disaster. I'd have to go to trial—by jury. That was the only way I could tell my story.

Before trial, I called the county attorney and asked for another opinion. "Hey, Brandon," I said. "The other day I got stopped and received a citation even though I was on duty trying to serve some papers. I see these patrol cars not giving turn signals and running red lights. Who knows if they're on duty? Can I stop these patrol cars and issue citations to them?"

"You bet," he said without hesitation. "So long as they're not running code."

I knew "running code" meant being on an official call. I filed that away for the next time I saw them violating the law.

The day of court finally arrived. I showed up and saw a grinning Tommy Haggerty on the other side. It was payback time.

We started the trial and things weren't going well. Every time I tried to tell my story, he'd cut me off and object. He asked the Gatesville police officer who had stopped me, "Is it everybody's responsibility to give a turn signal?"

"Oh, yes it is," he replied dutifully.

I found I could never get my story out. Shorty's former lawyer was tearing me up. I kept wondering where this talent had been when Shorty had handed him $2,500.

Tommy addressed the jury and told them, "Roger Hammack thinks he's above the law. But I'll tell you right now, it's everybody's responsibility to use a turn signal, whether it works or not."

I remember sitting there thinking, *With the evidence so far, heck—I'd find myself guilty.*

When the jury returned with a verdict, they did just that. I had to pay a $200 fine. The worst part was never getting to tell my story. That burned me deeply. The only way I'd be able to right this wrong was to turn back the hands of time and win that jury trial. That involved Einstein's Theory of General Relativity and something about quantum wormholes. I'd barely made a C in Astrophysics and Quantum Mechanics, so I was pretty sure I couldn't pull that off. When a friend suggested I write a book and tell my side of the story, that sounded much easier. As for Tommy Haggerty, eventually the city saw what I'd seen before the trial and they fired him.

Sometime after my disemboweling in court, I was in my personal vehicle—a truck with emergency lights, a radio, and everything I needed to be a patrol car—and driving through Gatesville, minding my business. Suddenly, I spotted a Gatesville patrol car making a right-hand turn without signaling. I passed the patrol car, watching it in my rearview mirror as it made a U-turn with no signals, no emergency lights, no nothing. I fell in behind and watched it for a while. It was just moseying along, in no hurry to be anywhere—certainly not on an official call. I reached down and flipped on my emergency lights. The patrol car didn't react. We traveled for half a mile and, still, the patrol car refused to pull over. I picked up the radio and called the Gatesville police dispatcher. "This is Constable Roger Hammack. I have a Gatesville patrol car that's not pulling over. Can you radio him?"

It took a minute, but suddenly, the patrol car hit its brake lights and pulled over.

At this point in the story, I want to take a moment and say to you, the reader, that pulling over a police car is a high-risk event. Should you ever decide to do this, I urge you to read on, absorbing the details and committing everything to memory while making sure your will is up to date.

With the patrol car stopped, I got out of my truck and walked up to the car. He had the window down and I recognized Lt. Don Norman's face. Don knew me too. I stuck out my hand and said, "My name is Roger Hammack. I'm the constable of Precinct 4. The reason I stopped you was that you just made two different turns with no turn signals. You all just got through prosecuting me for a no turn signal. So I'm just here to tell you that I could issue you a citation but I'm not going to. As a constable, I don't really write citations, so I'm not going to write you up."

Next thing I knew, that modern-day escalation cop monster emerged from the patrol car, screaming and hollering as loud as he could. Stunned, I stepped back and took it in, letting this volcano blow. At one point, he said, "You ever try to pull me over again, I'm not going to stop."

I made sure he was done before speaking. "Well, in that case, I'll have to take you to jail if you refuse to stop, because you'll be breaking the law."

"Let me tell you something—you ever try to stop me again, I'm going to put you down!"

I watched his hands for any quick movements. He might be looking for a chance to kill me. That's how mad he was. When he didn't make a move for his gun, I smiled and let it go, walking back to my truck.

A short while later, I called the Gatesville city manager and said, "Look, I need to have a meeting with you. Your police department's out of control."

"What do you mean out of control? I heard all about you stopping that lieutenant out there."

"Did he tell you he threatened to kill me?"

"No, he didn't. Come on down and we'll talk about it."

I went down there and told him the story. He said I needed to speak to the police chief.

"It does no good to talk to your chief," I said. "It's all one-sided. It's been like this ever since I've been constable. I called about people complaining and he always takes the side of the patrolmen. It'll do no good. I don't want to talk to him."

"No!" he insisted. "You need to go talk to him. I'll set up the meeting. Just go and talk to him."

I agreed and, five minutes later, he had the meeting set up—with an emphasis on *set up*.

I walked into Gatesville Police Department Chief Gholke's office. He was dressed in plain clothes. I looked around and noticed how it was the strangest-looking office I'd seen for law enforcement. There was absolutely nothing on the walls, only light-colored paint. It reminded me of walking into a mental health place, like one of the old state hospitals. Either he officed in a psych ward or this was not his real office.

We shook hands and sat down, discussing the situation.

"Roger," he said, "what you did was retaliation."

"It wasn't retaliation. Your guy broke the law and I had permission from Brandon Belt to pull him over. I can write citations if I want to."

We continued talking before Lieutenant Don Norman came in and said, "What you did out there got real close to retaliation."

"It wasn't, and I don't think you should be feeling that way," I responded.

"I don't remember what I said to you, but I didn't threaten to kill you."

"Well, you did," I insisted. "You threatened to put me down. When you say you're going to put something down like a dog, you're going to shoot it in the head with a gun. That's exactly what you said to me."

We went back and forth, with no progress made on anything. Finally, we all shook hands and I went home, setting down in writing exactly how my vehicles were detailed and showing how they were clearly marked. Then I mailed the letter to Chief Gholke and considered the matter settled.

It wasn't.

Not by a long shot.

CHAPTER EIGHTEEN

As Christmas approached, I had put the ticket incident behind me. I loved this time of year because it was a chance to spoil my grandchildren.

One day in December, I read in the paper that Leon River Mercantile, a western wear store in Gatesville, was having a midnight madness sale. Mary and I had been in the store several times before, shopping and purchasing some clothes. Also, I'd take my crew here every six months and buy them one pair of good work boots out of my own pocket. At $100 per pair and ten workers, I felt I'd been a loyal customer to this store. Now, it was under new ownership, so Mary and I wanted to look around to see if anything had changed. And we wanted to check out the inventory since we always bought our grandkids plenty of boots, hats, and shirts to ensure they stayed the best-looking grandkids in the world.

It was after dark when we pulled up in front of the store. I spotted a woman, Fonda Lee, and her male companion, Buck Long, entering the brightly lit building. Fonda and Buck had worked for me for a short while—maybe four months—before I'd let them go. Fonda had suffered a severe injury several years back when she'd worked for another outfit. Apparently, she'd been on a tractor pulling stumps with a chain connected to the tractor when it broke, hitting her in the head. She'd suffered brain damage and received a steel plate in her skull as a permanent reminder. She'd also lost one of her eyes, which was replaced with glass. As a result of all this damage, she had a hard time walking straight. Unfortunately, she also had a drinking problem. This made it tough to work. She was a very good person, helping anyone out, but she struggled with her drinking. If she could have controlled that, she would've been a great citizen and still working for me.

Fonda and I talked for bit near some shirt racks. I learned she was working for a framing crew and enjoying the work. I could tell she'd been drinking, but she was pleasant. We separated and I walked around with my wife as she picked up a few things to buy.

A few minutes later, I noticed law enforcement officer standing by the door. I squinted and saw it was Scott Williams, a Coryell County sheriff's deputy. He was off duty and working security for the store. As I came around the store, I walked up to him and shook his hand. "Hey, Scott, how are you doing today?" I asked.

He said he was good. I could tell he was watching for shoplifters, so I joined Mary at the cash register. After paying for the merchandise, I started for the exit when I noticed Scott talking to Fonda and Buck. As I drew closer, I could hear him. He was very rude, even threatening to take Fonda to jail. Then he started bullying her to the point she cowered down like a little puppy. I couldn't believe what I was seeing. Once again, the escalating cop was peeling off his clothes and turning into a law enforcement monster.

Scott continued on, saying she had been running into clothes racks and causing a disturbance, pointing and threatening jail three or four times. Then he switched tactics and reached a crescendo. "I could take you to jail. No, I'm *going* to take you to jail."

In Texas, every law enforcement officer is required to complete a crisis management course. Texas recognizes that escalation, bullying, and brute force are not always necessary to achieve the objective—which apparently in this case was simply getting Fonda to leave the store. I processed this situation in a split second. Perhaps Scott didn't know about Fonda's brain and vision injuries. Maybe somehow, he hadn't taken the crisis management course yet. I knew that the current Sheriff, Johnny Burks, had already suffered one suicide in the jail. I didn't want him to have another.

As someone who prides himself in de-escalation and calm law enforcement, I approached Scott to see if I could help. As I pulled a badge from my shirt pocket and showed it to Deputy Williams, I said slowly and politely, "You don't need to arrest anybody."

Then, just as I was about to describe Fonda's physical impairments, he interrupted me. "Get off my blacktop! Don't ever come up on my backside."

I stepped two feet away, confused, blinking at this sudden turn of events. I quickly glanced down at the vinyl tile to see if I had somehow made it to the parking lot and was standing on asphalt. I wasn't.

Since he wasn't making sense, I was about to ask another question when Deputy Williams yelled at me, going crazy with rage. That monster had emerged in full.

At this point, I reminded myself that I was an elected constable. I'd given an oath to protect the citizens of Coryell County. I needed to stop this abusive policing.

I tried talking but he kept cutting me off, pointing a finger at my chest. Seeing that finger lit my fuse. I raised my voice and ripped off a few cuss words. As we were standing there, my wife grabbed my arm and said, "Let's go. Let's get out of here. We don't want to have a mess."

As Mary and I walked from the store, I called Sheriff Burks and advised him of the situation. I also spotted Fonda and Buck going to their vehicle, with Buck driving. Thankfully, we all left without getting arrested or shot.

The next day, I went back to the store and asked to talk with the new owners. The salesclerk said they weren't in. When I asked for the phone number, she wouldn't give it to me. I told the clerk that I wanted to pass on some information that the lady they'd had a problem with had severe physical and mental problems. I asked them to call me, but they never did. I didn't know why until much later.

I discussed everything with Mary and we decided to never go back into the store. There were better—*safer*—places to shop.

173

Several days later, I got to thinking about the incident and Scott Williams. Perhaps I hadn't handled it the way I should have. Even though I felt Scott wasn't practicing good law enforcement, I still wanted to apologize to him.

In mid-December, I was in the justice building. Standing in the hallway next to my office, I spotted Scott Williams at the far end of the hall. "Hey, Scott, come down here a minute," I said politely.

As he made the fifteen-foot walk, I stuck out my hand. "Hey, Scott. I'm sorry about the other night at Leon Mercantile. I'd like to apologize to you."

He frowned. "Reluctantly, I will accept your apology. But don't let it happen again."

I began explaining why I had reacted and tried to detail Fonda's injuries, but, just like in the store, he cut me off, not wanting to hear anything. (It seems refusal to listen to someone's side of the story is a rampant disease in Coryell County.)

I gave up trying to explain Fonda's brain damage and glass eye and said, "Well, you know, we were both a little bit wrong down there that night."

That's when he said in a loud, rough voice, "Man, you are a prick, aren't you?"

Obviously, someone had been talking behind my back, telling him how terrible I was. This meant the escalation game had returned. Not only was he refusing to listen to my side, but he'd called me a prick. He should have been working in pyrotechnics, because he knew how to light my fuse.

"If you want to be an ass, then get the fuck out of my office!" I yelled.

By this time, he was standing in the doorway, blocking an exit from my office. Scott is close to seven feet tall and 300 pounds. He's a massive guy, someone who could play pro football. I am just five-eight and 180 pounds. I'd have no chance against a giant like this.

I attempted to leave, but he wouldn't budge. I waited for him to move, yet he refused, forcing me to attempt to squeeze around him. I couldn't make it, so I called out for Marvin Wills. Marvin was a Special Ranger for the Texas Cattlemen's Association and had an office near mine. Marvin came over to us and I said, "Marvin would you get him out of here?"

Marvin said, "Well, I can't force him to leave because it's a public building, but I will ask him to leave. If he agrees, I'll escort him to the door."

Marvin turned to Scott. "Would you be willing to leave?"

Scott smirked. "Yeah, I'll leave."

Together, they walked to the door.

Marvin came back to his office and sat down in a chair. I walked in and said, "Marvin, I'm sorry about using that language out here."

"Don't worry about it, Roger," he said. "But you need to watch your language around the girls up front."

The girls up front were court clerks.

"You're right," I told him. "I had a problem with Williams at the Leon Mercantile store."

"I know all about it. Those folks that own the store are good friends of mine."

I stopped talking because I could tell someone had already gotten to him. Marvin wasn't going to listen to my side of the story, because the trial had already been held and judgment passed in my absence. I guessed I was the loser.

"Well, I didn't know them," was all I could manage before heading back to my office.

I went up front to speak to the girls. Laura Smith, who was a very sweet person and always alert to what was going on in the building, was there. "I'm sorry about my language I used back down the hall."

"Aw, don't worry about it," she said.

175

"It will never happen again."

As I spoke to Laura, Marvin brushed past me, walking over to the sheriff's office. I knew they were very good friends, so I assumed they needed to match up their stories to make sure I was the bad guy.

As I left the building, I told Sheriff Burks that I'd tried to apologize to Scott Williams, but it hadn't worked out. The sheriff said he was sorry. I'd find out later what he was sorry about.

At this point, I didn't fully recognize the enemies who were springing up from the ground to go against me. From the ticket incident to the Leon Mercantile fiasco to the Scott Williams confrontation, I was signing my death warrant. I should've seen it coming, but I was the one who spent the day trying to help people—not screaming, bullying, and body slamming them to the ground. That's why this last incident was all my enemies needed to tighten the noose and pull the lever, releasing the trap door.

It all started the spring of 2006, long before any of these incidents. I received a call from a lady in Hamilton County who wanted to talk to me about building a fence. I drove to her property and met the woman—Laura Howard. She took me into the house and sat me down. What I learned completely amazed me.

Laura lived on this ranch with her husband, Harvey Howard, and her sister Carol Krist. All three were senior citizens. I sat at their kitchen table as they explained how each one of them had grown up on farms and ranches and wanted to own a ranch before they died. They'd put their money together and bought this nice ranch. Now, they were living their dreams.

When I first met them, they had been on the ranch for about a year. They showed me around the spread, telling me how much garbage they had cleaned up and hauled away. They also pointed to a four-car carport they had built by themselves with no help. They had welded it and done everything. And these folks were in their late sixties!

I was thoroughly impressed with them and how far they'd come.

"Roger," Laura said, "now that we've cleared out the junk and brush, we need a fence built so we can get some cows. Can you help us with that?"

"Of course," I said. "That's what I love doing." We agreed on a price and I made the arrangements to get started.

A few weeks later, we had built two miles of six-strand barbed wire. We also built a set of working pens and repaired the barn. While I was out there, we became great friends.

After we finished that job, they called me anytime they needed help. One time, they wanted a fence around a burn-pit. If it was a job that needed a crew, I'd charge them for the job. If it was something I could handle myself, a glass of iced tea was all the payment I accepted. I really liked those three and helped them out any way I could.

A few years after the first job, I learned Harvey had passed away. It was very hard on the two sisters to maintain the ranch. Laura started going downhill shortly after Harvey passed. She had to go into a nursing home and sure enough, she passed away. This left Carol alone on the ranch, with all the obligations that came with it. I'd go by and check on her periodically, to see if she needed any help.

Laura's son had inherited two-thirds of the ranch when she died. He worked in the oil industry and was looking for some tax write-offs. He made a deal with Carol: he'd furnish all the labor, equipment, and everything needed to maintain the ranch if Carol would leave him the ranch. She agreed, and life smoothed out for Carol. But something unexpected happened: Laura's son died, leaving the ranch and all the equipment to Carol. She thought she could still handle the workload, but she couldn't. She had to do something.

Carol called me one day and asked if I could find somebody to take the cows to sale and lease the ranch for grazing. I called a good friend of mine, Mark Carothers. He went out there and bought the cows on sight, taking them to sale. Then he leased the land and brought some of his old rough-looking cows out there to maintain the agricultural exemption. That solved Carol's problems. With me checking on her, repairing a fence, fertilizing a field, or removing a downed tree, it looked like she could stay there to the bitter end.

One day, I received a surprising call from Carol, who was living in Fort Worth. "Hey, Roger," she said, "I sold that ranch and we've already closed on it. The people gave me a thirty-day lease to stay there and get all my stuff off. I need to get out there and haul off the tractor and blue pickup. Can you get those for me?"

"Of course," I said. "How soon would you like me to do that?"

"Right away," she replied. "My son is living out there and I don't trust him. Can you tell him that the new owners will be there next week so he needs to move?"

I listened carefully and swallowed hard. Her son, William, had been in and out of prison, with a long line of problems—most of them stemming from drugs. I questioned her more about this situation.

"Roger, I've given him almost thirteen thousand dollars to find another place. He won't be left in the cold."

"Yeah, I'll go get everything," I told her. "And I'll relay the message."

As I've said before, I wear my gun and badge most of the time in case I stop to help somebody. Every cop knows our shift never ends. Even when we're off duty, we might have to respond to a problem. If you were being beaten by a robber, would you be happy if I stood across the street and let it happen? "Hey, I'm off duty. Call nine-one-one and let them handle it—*if* you survive this beating."

I don't think so. That's why I had decals on my personal vehicle that read "Roger Hammack, Constable of Coryell County." People who needed help would know I was in law enforcement and not there to hurt them. With that said, I was in my pickup truck on this particular day, carrying Shorty and another hand with me. They were on my payroll, so the county would have nothing to do with this. I was "off duty," and doing it as a favor to an elderly woman.

Since I was coming into Hamilton County, I called the sheriff's office. "My name is Roger Hammack. I'm a constable in Coryell

County. I'm coming over to pick up a tractor for a friend, but I don't think I'll need any help doing it. I'm just going to pick it up and haul it to my ranch for safekeeping."

They were fine with that, so I proceeded to the ranch. When I arrived, I found Carol's two daughters there in a car. One of them, Carolyn, also brought along her husband, Randy. The other was Tina Bauman. Then I noticed a deputy there. That was common. I went up to the deputy and greeted him, explaining what was happening. I was talking to him when William, Carol's son, came up to us. I took the opportunity to tell him the new owners were coming and he needed to move.

"Well, it's going to take a long time," he said, grinning.

I knew from his reply that he was possession-savvy. Folks who've been through the system learn that if they have permission to be on the property, they can stay until owners force them off through an eviction. From the filing of the lawsuit, to the trial and through a long appeal, he could drag this out for months before he'd have to move. It was clear he intended to avail himself of that extra time.

"Okay," I said, glancing over at the two daughters. "We're here to take the tractor and the truck. We'll be out of your hair pretty quickly."

I walked over to the daughters and explained that he'd have to be evicted. "The best thing you can do is call the new owners and have them come down from Austin right now and file eviction papers. I'll tell them what they need to do."

When William indicated that the tractor and truck were staying, things shifted. He knew his mother wanted the equipment off the ranch so she could sell it herself. Obviously, he had his owns plans for the equipment.

Carolyn and Tina didn't want to leave until the new owners arrived from Austin. They wanted to explain to them what was going on. They tried reasoning with their brother, urging him to cooperate and leave. After all, his mother had been good to him. He had plenty of money. Still, he refused. That's when voices raised.

I watched as William started bullying them around. He even lunged at them before I stepped in between them. I looked around for the deputy, but he had just left. I guess he was scared or didn't want to see what happened next.

Left by myself to handle this mess, I said calmly but firmly, "Boy, if you cause any problem out here, I'm going to arrest you. I can do that because I can serve a warrant anywhere in the state of Texas."

That just bounced right off him. This guy had been to prison and was a pro. He wasn't afraid of anything.

Here we stood, no one leaving or giving an inch. As they continued yelling at each other, I called the sheriff's department and asked for help, telling them I had a domestic situation. I held the phone away from my ear, not believing what I heard. A deputy told me it was a civil matter and they weren't getting involved. Recall earlier that when a cop says it's a civil matter, it means they don't have to work the case.

"Your car was broken into? You have insurance so let them handle it. *It's a civil matter.*"

"Your tenant is destroying your property? *It's a civil matter.* Go to court."

I knew full well that some domestic situations escalated to injuries and even death. For sure, they became criminal matters. Sadly, more officers are killed answering domestic calls than any other call.

Truthfully, when the arguing started, I didn't want to be out there. But I knew in my heart that it would turn violent. If I left the scene, someone would be hurt or killed. How I wished that the elected officials of Hamilton County had decided to stay out there. Instead, all I could think of was how these lazy cowards had left me in a bad spot. I was on my own, and no one was coming to help.

CHAPTER NINETEEN

I wracked my brain for a solution. William knew his days were numbered and his mother wanted to sell the equipment for money to live on. He had no incentive to leave and every reason to stay. I decided to make a generous offer to him, something that could break this logjam.

"You know, William, I'll get my crew and help you move. I won't even charge you anything for it."

"No thanks," he replied, mouth twitching.

"Okay, I've got my truck and trailer. Let me get that tractor first. Then I'll get the truck."

He stepped forward, puffing up his chest. "You can't take the tractor and you can't take the truck. I'm not leaving, so make me."

I'm sure my jaw dropped. As I collected myself, I stood there staring at him, contemplating the options. He was getting agitated and looked like he was high. Since everyone was huddled in cars, I left him there and started looking around. I figured he wouldn't stop me.

I checked around the barn and saw the tractor and the truck, but couldn't find a separate piece of equipment—a backhoe—that Carol was also worried about. Making a large circle around the outside of the structures, I still did not see the backhoe. That's the moment I realized stuff was missing.

I found William and asked him about the backhoe. He refused to tell me what had happened to it. I shook my head and left him standing there.

Walking back to Carolyn and Tina, I relayed the information. They were distraught. This would cost their mother much-needed money. I punched my thigh as my anger at the sheriff's office came to a head. If they would have just done their job, the problem would have been solved by now. I decided to try them one more time.

I reached a deputy and told him about the missing backhoe. "I think there are other things walking off this ranch. It's turning domestic. You need to come out here and talk to these people."

"Whyyyyy?" the deputy said sarcastically in an up and down voice, drawing out the why.

Once again, I couldn't believe the lack of professionalism from Hamilton County law enforcement. "Because these people need some help. That's why!"

I'll give the deputy credit. When he decided not to help someone, he stayed with it. There was no changing his mind. The only option left for the two sisters was to leave and file a report with the sheriff that the backhoe had been stolen. Carolyn left with Randy to go into town, leaving Tina behind. In no time, the couple returned.

"What happened?" I asked Carolyn.

"The sheriff refused to take our complaint. Said it was a civil matter."

"Yeah," I said. "If there's no crime, there's no need to get off my butt and investigate. Just like Chief Banks told me, 'Cops love staying at the station.'"

But I had one more card up my sleeve: a property hearing. Justice of the Peace courts have jurisdiction to hear property disputes. All Carolyn had to do was go into town to the J.P. court and file the papers. This would cause the constable to come out and seize the property. It was a good plan.

I sent Carolyn off by herself to take care of that. Meanwhile, we started loading the pickup truck on my flatbed. William watched, but didn't stop us. When it was done, I told William it was time to load the tractor. That's when he sprinted to it, started the engine, and took off, flooring the accelerator. I believed he was driving the tractor impaired, but I didn't have any testing gear. I also knew the sheriff would disagree with my opinion. That's why I sent Randy alone in his car after William. I told him to see where he was going, because I had yet another idea.

I had a friend in the Coryell County Auto Theft division. I knew all these counties worked together on stolen equipment. Even though this was in a neighboring county, I wondered if he could help.

"Look, Sparky," I said, "I've got a problem over here in Hamilton County. The sheriff won't do anything about it. And there's a backhoe missing out here with a guy who just drove off on a tractor. He's stealing it."

"Well, that would be up to Hamilton County," he said. "Deputy Carroway is the one who handles auto theft over there. Why don't you call him? Let me give you his number."

I hung up and called Deputy Carroway a couple times, but he didn't answer. He worked for the same Hamilton County Sheriff's Department, so it wasn't too surprising. (It's been several years and I'm still waiting for him to return those calls.) As I hung up a third time, my phone rang. It was Carolyn.

"Did you get the property hearing papers filed?" I asked her.

"No. The judge refused to take them. Said the value of the tractor was over the jurisdictional limit."

"Oh, for crying out loud!" I knew the tractor was worth $35,000 and the limit was $10,000. I had figured it was up to William to object to it, not for a judge to reject the filing outright. As I thought about all this, I called Carol in Fort Worth and made her an offer of $15,000 for the tractor. She accepted, and I had a plan.

When Randy returned, he drove me to the spot where William had driven the tractor. I grinned. It was parked in the yard of a person known to me. I'd known this person for a long time, as he'd stolen a lot of property. He was also good at moving stolen property to people who could pay for it. And he had a big heart. If your car broke down and you needed help, he'd be right there. Unfortunately, when you came back, your car would be gone. But other than that, he was a great guy.

I jumped out of the car and hustled up to this person. "Listen here," I said, "this tractor that William brought you, I just purchased it from the owner who lives in Fort Worth. I'm waiting on the bill of sale. I don't want nothing to happen to this tractor because I'm filing for a property hearing. You might win it in court, but as of right now, I own it—so make sure nothing happens to it."

He understood that I was on to him.

Randy and I left this scene and returned to the ranch, still waiting for one of the new owners from Austin. Eventually, a woman arrived.

Carolyn and I explained the situation: that William refused to leave the property and he was removing equipment off the ranch.

"What are my options?" she asked me.

"You need to file for eviction at the justice of the peace court," I told her. "But there's one thing you need to do or they'll throw the eviction case out. You need to go over there and put a little note on the door, giving William three days to vacate the property. It's in the statutes. You have to do that."

She wrote one out and posted it on the door while we watched, making sure nothing happened to her.

Before I left the property, Sheriff Bewley called me. At this point, I'd been out there eight hours trying to get the situation resolved. Bewley wanted to know what the hell I was doing out there as a constable. I stared down at my notes, including the twenty-five pages of William's criminal history.

"I'm not out here as a constable," I told him. "I'm out here just trying to help these people. This guy is stealing a tractor and everything off this ranch."

His voice rose. "Roger, I'm telling you, I'm the sheriff of Hamilton County!"

For once, I decided it was my time to cut someone off. "Just kiss my ass! I'll get Texas Rangers to come out here and get that tractor."

I hung up and decided I'd had enough for one day. Everyone was exhausted, so we all left the property.

Later on that same night, Carolyn and Tina went back out to the ranch to get a few little knickknacks. This wasn't a smart thing to do, because William was out there. Sure enough, he came running at them while they sat in the car. According to Carolyn, he proceeded to beat on the car, threatening them. Fortunately, they escaped unharmed and called me, along with the sheriff's office. I hung up and called the sheriff's office myself. "If you aren't going out there to make sure no one gets hurt, I will."

"We're sending a deputy out there now," they told me.

Finally, the Hamilton County Sheriff's Department was actually doing something.

The next morning, Carolyn called to fill me in on what had happened when the deputy arrived. She said the deputy had spent more time getting information on them than on going down to the house and checking on William, who was running through the woods with a gun. It seemed like William had the golden ticket of freedom in Hamilton County.

No sooner had I finished talking to Carolyn than the new owner called. She'd just learned that Hamilton County had served the eviction papers on William. I shook my head at their incompetence. By law, they couldn't serve the papers for three days. This would give William a guaranteed victory in court—*if* he showed up in court and *if* he raised the issue.

It turned out William *did* show up for the eviction, but *didn't* raise the issue. He lost. Still, he wasn't going anywhere. He knew the system well. The new owner was forced to go back down to court and file a writ of possession. When she had that in hand, I went out the next day and waited for the Hamilton County Sheriff's Department to enforce it. Yet William was long gone. A deputy drove up,

185

walked around the house, got into his car, and was about to leave when I went over to him. "Why are you guys acting so scared out here? Why don't you want to help these people?"

"Well, it's a civil matter and we can't get involved," he replied.

"It might be a civil matter, and it might also be a criminal matter," I said, frustrated.

I was completely dumbfounded. Why were they treating this habitual criminal like he owned Hamilton County? Did William have something on Hamilton County or any of the law enforcement officers? I wondered.

I got on the phone and called the Texas Rangers, reporting the missing backhoe and the tractor in the possession of the person known to me. I was assigned to Jason Bobo, the Ranger who worked Coryell County. He had me sit in his pickup truck and tell him everything that had happened. When I finished, I was sure he'd get busy and start looking for that stolen backhoe.

A few hours later, Ranger Bobo called and said he had the tractor now.

"Okay," I said, "get Hamilton County to set up the property hearing and we'll be there."

He said he would put the tractor in storage. Finally, someone was doing something to help this old woman. Hopefully, he would find that missing backhoe.

A few weeks later, Ranger Bobo called and said he wanted to interview the two helpers I had out there at the ranch. I assumed this was part of his investigation into the missing backhoe. I gave him the information and he interviewed the man first. After he interviewed Shorty, he told her she had an arrest warrant for something in Hamilton County and took her in. A coworker of hers collected her pay from me and took it to the jail to bond her out. I spoke with Ranger Bobo and asked if he'd found out anything on that backhoe.

"Roger, we don't know what kind it is, or the color or nothing."

I told him I'd contact the owner and see what I could find out. Sure enough, I received a photo of it by text a few days later and forwarded it to Bobo. Hopefully, this would get things moving.

A week later, I found a witness who would testify in court that the person known to me had helped William sell the backhoe and was paid $500. I forwarded that to Bobo, certain this was the break we needed.

The summer had finally arrived. So had lush vegetation and hot temperatures—a Texas specialty. The mosquitos weren't too bad, but the crickets were sure making a racket. Still, I loved this time of year.

It had been about four months since the backhoe had disappeared. I hadn't heard from Ranger Bobo for a while. I hoped he hadn't given up on the investigation because an old lady would surely be disappointed.

It was July 2, a Thursday night, when Mary and I had a big family reunion planned. All my brothers and sisters were coming to our ranch, "It'll Do." We'd been planning this for six months and I wanted everything to be perfect.

My siblings arrived the day before, staying in hotels in Gatesville. A great friend of mine, Benjamin (Benji) Johnson, owned J & M Hill Country Bar-B-Q. He was in my backyard preparing a large meal for everyone. Besides the steaks Benji had brought, we were serving lamb chops and burgers from the ranch. Mary and I greeted our guests, making sure they were having a good time while Benji cooked up the food.

Around 6:30, Benji told me the food was ready. I started making my way through the crowd, telling everyone to take a seat. It was time to eat.

As I was doing this, my phone rang. I pulled it out and saw the name Jason Bobo.

I thought about letting it go to voicemail, but we were never off duty. I punched the talk button. "Hey, how you doing there?" I said to him.

"Oh, I'm doing good, Roger. Can you come down here to the office a minute? I need to talk to you."

I looked at the guests taking their seats. "I'm getting ready to sit down and have supper with my family. Give me about thirty minutes and I'll be down there."

"Naw," he said, "you need to come on down. Let's get this taken care of right quick."

I shook my head. All these months, and he had to deal with the stolen backhoe right now? That was crazy. Still, I agreed to come into town. Carol was counting on me.

I told Mary, who was disappointed, and she told our guests I'd be right back. I jumped in my pickup truck and headed to Gatesville. On the way down there, I thought about the stolen tractor. We'd gone through the court system and had it returned to Carol. It was a successful ending to a traumatic event. Hopefully, Bobo had good news on the backhoe.

I parked across from the courthouse and walked over. When I found Bobo in his office, I shook his hand. "Whatcha got?"

"Roger, we had a grand jury meeting over this incident in Hamilton County and they came back with an indictment."

I smiled, because Ranger Bobo had found the criminal and solved the case. I knew he'd show up those incompetent fools in Hamilton County. Carol would be so happy.

"Great," I said. "Who's the culprit?"

He held up a piece of paper. "You. I got a warrant for your arrest."

"What?!" I exclaimed, completely stunned. "On what?"

"Giving a false statement and presenting a false document." He picked up a thick file and thrust it at me. "I've been working on this case for three months."

"I don't understand," was all I could manage. Stunned and confused, I considered for a brief moment that this might be an elaborate practical joke. I knew I didn't have the missing backhoe.

"Did you tell a person that sometimes you can bluff someone?"

"No," I said, having no idea what he was talking about.

"Okay. Turn around."

I was having an out-of-body experience. This couldn't be happening. My family had been in law enforcement and served this county since the beginning. I wasn't some dirty cop stealing a petty backhoe.

I winced as I heard the handcuffs click around my wrists. I couldn't believe this was America.

He walked me across the street to the Coryell County Jail. In the profession, we call this the perp walk. Cops love doing the perp walk with high-profile criminals like celebrities and CEOs. The patrol car will stop in the parking spot farthest from the jail so the cameras can see the suspect make the long walk in handcuffs. If they're really mean, they'll hook up those leg chains so the suspect can only walk ten inches at a time. I glanced around and didn't see any press. That was odd, since it was clear someone had it in for me.

I entered the jail, a place I knew well. I had taken a lot of folks here, never thinking for one second I'd be an occupant. Fortunately, though, the jailers were very respectful to me.

After a while, they called me up to go through the line. I was booked and fingerprinted. Then they took my mug shot. That was a sobering moment.

Bail was set at $10,000 by a district judge with a PR bond granted. However, Judge John Lee came down and signed some paperwork which granted my release with just my promise that I would show up for trial. That was a blessing. With that done, I should have been out of there right then. But there was a computer glitch so I stayed in jail for *three* extra hours while they tried to fix it—I guess.

I thought about Ranger Bobo's only question: "Did you say you could sometimes bluff someone?" What did that mean? Was he referring to the time a criminal came at me with a ten-inch butcher knife and I'd convinced him to drop it so I didn't have to kill him? Yeah, I guess I'd bluffed him.

Then I remembered the undercover work I did, getting beat up and chipping a tooth. I guess I'd bluffed some drug dealers into selling me drugs.

The more I thought about it, the more convinced I was that I had pressed the wrong buttons. Was William being protected by the Hamilton sheriff's office for some reason? Was that person known to me a valuable person to law enforcement? Had this backhoe ended up on some important person's farm or ranch and they didn't want Roger Hammack sniffing around for it? What was I missing?

I had heard stories from undercover cops about detectives who were arrested and indicted on false charges because they'd been investigating a drug operation that was paying dirty cops for protection. Had I stumbled onto something like that? Or was the cold hard truth that I was a big-time criminal who needed to be locked up in prison?

I pondered all of this as I sat watching the jailers stare at the computer, hoping it would start working. What a nightmare.

By the time I got back to the ranch, everyone was gone. And it turned out I'd missed the last meal I'd have with my sister, Rebecca Nell. She came down with Alzheimer's and doesn't know who I am. Missing something like that—man, that's hard to forgive.

As I tried going to sleep, tossing and turning, I kept wondering if the end times were near—when right becomes wrong and wrong becomes right. Were cops going to be the ones in prison while criminals were celebrated with statues? Would illegal drugs and criminal activities become legal? I knew an innocent person could go to prison. Could an innocent cop join him?

CHAPTER TWENTY

I sat in my office, staring out the window as the shadows crossed the field. I'd been here all day and felt completely exhausted. "Do you have enough, Tim?"

He looked through his thick pad of notes. "I'd say. Let me get some discovery and talk to the D.A. See where we stand on this. Why don't we knock off for the day?"

"Sounds good," I said, looking forward to sitting in my easy chair with a cup of coffee in my hand.

I walked Tim to the door and watched him leave. My brain was complete mush. Spilling your life story out over eight hours tends to do that to a person. That's why I was overjoyed to see Mary with a fresh mug of coffee.

"Are you okay?" she asked.

"I don't know. One day, you think you're a good person, helping people and mentoring kids. The next day, you're an accused felon."

Mary moved in close. "It's not like it's been in the past, when a man would try to beat you at the ballot box. Now, the goal is to get you arrested."

I hoped she was wrong, but feared she was right. Maybe a good night's sleep would change my perspective.

A few days later, a Monday morning, I awoke tired and irritable. Dressing for work, I received a call from Sheriff Johnny Burks. He wanted to talk to me before I started my day. I hustled into his office and spotted a deputy hiding in the corner, as if there might be trouble. That wasn't a good sign.

Sheriff Burks emerged from behind his desk and shoved a thick packet of papers into my chest. "Roger, this is for you. Consider yourself served."

I turned away from him, not wanting to give him the satisfaction of seeing me suffer. I went to my office, sat at my desk, and read the complaint. The headline on the first page caught my attention: *Petition For Removal*. The county attorney had filed a suit to remove me from office. I felt my blood pressure rise as I turned each page. It was littered with lies. And there were sixty-plus pages of it.

It took me a while, but when I finished reading the lawsuit, I knew I would win this fight. Bobo's main argument was that I'd tried to illegally evict Carol's son and seize property without the proper papers. This was dead wrong. Carol had the paperwork and a bill of sale to the tractor and had not given her son permission to drive or remove it from the property. I couldn't imagine the stupidity of someone in law enforcement thinking there was no crime when someone removed property without the owner's permission.

As every law enforcement officer should know, the Texas Penal Code is chock-full of ways to commit theft. When I'd started in the early seventies, taking property you didn't own had been the only way to be convicted of theft. But later, when I'd gone to Alaska, the Texas legislature reorganized and expanded the penal code. Section 31—the chapter covering theft—was heavily revised. Now, if you didn't technically steal someone's property but secreted it, like slipping it into a trash dumpster (where you'd later "find" it), you were guilty of theft. The penal code had words like "deprived," which was defined as disposing of property in a manner that makes recovery by the owner unlikely.

What had Bobo (or anyone else in Hamilton County) thought when William Alexander drove the tractor to the house of a known property thief/fence? Was Bobo aware of Sec. 31.01(2)(C)? Had

Bobo even investigated if Alexander had the title? I didn't think so, because Carol Krist had the title in her possession. And it was made out in her name. If Carol was lying about that, she could be arrested for making a false report to a law enforcement officer. Since Bobo hadn't arrested Carol, it was obvious he believed she had a bill of sale.

The Texas Penal Code was a sharp knife, honed by decades of technicalities. Prosecutors had seen too many thieves slip through loopholes. For example, in the olden days, a thief would steal a vehicle, then drive it to a parking lot where witnesses would see a second person get in and drive it away. If we stopped the car with the second person driving, we couldn't prove they stole the car because they hadn't. We'd have to prove they were in a conspiracy to steal it, which needed the first guy. The revised penal code fixed that. The theft section now had something called "Unauthorized Use of a Motor Vehicle." In simple terms, if you were caught operating a *motor-propelled* vehicle without the consent of the owner, you were guilty of a felony. That's exactly what William Alexander had been doing when he'd driven it off the ranch. Apparently, some law enforcement officers didn't know a tractor was a motor-propelled vehicle. In fact, the Texas Transportation Code had strict require-ments for tractors to have headlights and reflectors. Why? Because they are often driven on the roads where cars are too.

Another part of the penal code covered that time when you gave your neighbor consent to borrow your lawnmower but he failed to return it. When I was a rookie, because you gave him consent to possess it, you were sunk. You had to go to civil court. Now, Texas allowed you to withdraw consent and turn your neighbor into a thief and thus be arrested. Even if Carol had initially given Alexander consent to drive the tractor, she'd withdrawn it the day I'd arrived with his sisters. They'd made it clear he couldn't drive or possess the tractor. This was Law Enforcement 101.

The crazy part in all this was that the stolen tractor had ended up at the home of a known thief. And guess what? The penal code had that covered too. Section 31.03(c)(1) allowed evidence of other stolen property transactions the buyer had participated in. So did Texas Rule of Evidence 404(b)(2), which allowed prior crimes and wrongful acts to show that you intended to buy stolen property. The past of the person known to me could have been used at trial against him and Alexander.

I could go on and on with this, including operating a motor vehicle while intoxicated, which I believed Alexander fit under. But really, Bobo, as a Texas Ranger, and the sheriff's deputies of Hamilton County should've known this. After all, the training and tests we'd taken to get our law enforcement licenses were the same for all of us. I know. I'd studied hard. I had to learn all this minutiae. Hadn't they?

I gathered up the packet and ran to my lawyer's office. I needed to show him this new bundle of pain.

"Roger, I was just about to call you," Tim said, emerging from his office. "I have more information on your indictment."

"Good. And I just got served with a petition to remove me from office," I said, handing him the packet.

He held the lawsuit in his palm, weighing it. "This is pretty thick. I'm sure it tracks with the information I have."

"Which is?"

"Bobo recorded you from the moment you met with him. He wasn't trying to recover any stolen property. He was investigating you from first contact."

"That's what I just read," I said, plopping down in a chair in front of his desk. "It was a setup. They weren't interested in any stolen property or possible violence. They put the red dot on my chest and ignored the rest."

Tim took his place behind his desk and nodded. "And Bobo put the Western Wear incident with Scott Williams in there to slap you around a bit. For good measure, he added the traffic stop with the Gatesville Police Department. Anything to tar and feather you. But the good news is I've found a bunch of holes in their case and I'm just getting started. Sit down and let's go over it."

An hour later, I felt much better. Tim was in control of this mess. The only issue I had was the mention of legal fees. I suddenly owed him a new retainer to handle the removal suit. If the case lasted long enough, I'd be short on cash. I needed to review my financial situation with Mary and see how long we could last.

Four days after I had been arrested, I ran into Sheriff Johnny Burks— the man who had served me with the removal lawsuit.

"That thing is full of lies," I told him. "Why didn't you come and ask for my side of the story?"

He held up his hands. "Hey, all I did was serve the lawsuit. I had nothing to do with it."

I couldn't believe what I was hearing. "But you're the top law enforcement officer in the county. Don't you think you should've investigated these claims? Just a tiny bit?"

His back stiffened. "When you're sheriff, you can do whatever you want."

He spun on his heel and walked away, as angry as I felt. Yet another law enforcement officer who didn't want to look into the facts. *Strange.*

I made my way home, where Mary greeted me with an online article about how I'd been arrested. It was from Waco. As I read it, I noticed the author was Wilma Haggerty. Talk about revenge. Her husband, Tommy Haggerty, was the lawyer who'd messed up Shorty's custody battle with her mom. Then, he'd been the city attorney who'd prosecuted me for the traffic violation. I'd told him he was worthless. Now, his wife was getting in the act. As a member of the media, she could hammer me all she wanted to.

As I read her article, I noticed she had talked to the Coryell District Attorney and County Attorney. For some reason, she hadn't had time to call me for a quote. *Strange.*

When you hear people talk about bias in the media, this is a good example. How hard would it have been for her to find my number and put in a call? If I'd failed to call her back, she would've been on solid ground to write, "Messages left to Roger Hammack were not returned." Instead, by not making the call, she didn't have to worry about hearing a different side of the story, one that would hurt her attack piece.

This is the evil that's out there. Once the red dot lands on your chest, everyone pulls the trigger and lets the facts catch up later.

A week after this, Tim and I met again. By now, he had received all the discovery in the case. The first thing he noticed was the date of the grand jury.

"They indicted you on June twenty-third and your bond was set that same day—June twenty-third. Yet Bobo held that indictment for *ten* days. You're supposed to be a dirty cop. Why would he wait so long?"

I thought carefully about this. "You don't think he was waiting to arrest me at my ranch, do you?"

"What do you mean?"

I explained the family reunion at my ranch on the day he arrested me. Everyone in town knew my family had flown in to attend it. The festivities were no secret. "I can only assume Bobo's plan was to call me just as we were sitting down for dinner, certain I wouldn't answer the phone. Most law enforcement officials would've let it go to voicemail. But I always answer my phone. It's my job. My work ethic. I think he wanted to drive to my ranch and arrest me in front of my family. Maybe the press would've been there. Maybe someone was watching from the road and saw me about to serve dinner. Otherwise, why wait? I wouldn't have waited on a dirty cop. No telling what other crimes would be committed or how many more people the cop could hurt."

"That makes sense," Tim said, picking up a packet of papers. "And the suit to remove you from office was filed June twenty-sixth, again before you were arrested. Sheriff Burks or anyone else had plenty of time to ask for your side of the story, but they didn't. They wanted to spring it on you."

Hearing this made me angry. When Tim told me he'd discovered that the grand jury had seen only a tiny slice of documents from Bobo's report—a cherry-picking of anything that made me look bad—I grew hot. I wondered how the grand jury members would've voted with my side of the story.

I returned to the ranch with something nagging me in the back of my mind. Going over my notes, I focused on the stolen tractor. When we had been at the ranch dealing with Alexander, Carolyn had driven to town to file for a property hearing in the justice of the peace court. This was in Hamilton County. Rather than let the case proceed to the judge, the court clerks had denied her access to the court by refusing to take her filing. When I'd asked Bobo to set up a property hearing for the stolen tractor, I assumed he would file it in the *county* court of Hamilton County, since it had higher jurisdictional limits than the justice court. Yet somehow, he'd been able to file it in the same JP court that had rejected Carolyn. I wasn't a lawyer, but this didn't make sense. It was very *strange*.

When we'd had the property hearing weeks later, a visiting judge heard the case because the elected judge recused himself. Why did he do that? Why did we need a different judge? That too was *strange*.

Carol won the case when she explained she had clear title and had given my check back. She was the rightful owner, which meant she was able to take and sell the tractor for valuable money she needed to live on. That was the right outcome.

I leaned back in my chair, staring up at the ceiling. The thought of the missing backhoe wouldn't leave my mind. No one had found it yet. And every time I went looking for it, I got punched in the face. First it was Hamilton County's refusal to help me with the situation at Carol's ranch. They didn't care about it because they were focused on investigating me as a dirty cop. Then Bobo interviewed one of my crew members, Shorty, and arrested her when he was done. Next thing I knew, the Coryell County District Attorney indicted me. And the Coryell County Attorney filed a lawsuit to remove me.

Why?

Who had this backhoe?

Was it the tip of some iceberg of corruption in Coryell and Hamilton counties, or was I just dreaming up some wild conspiracy?

On July 11, the local paper ran a front-page article with my mug shot. It was both embarrassing and humiliating. I couldn't believe that a life filled with helping people had led me to this. Meanwhile, my lawyer filed paperwork in the civil case to dismiss the allegations. He stated because I wasn't acting in my official capacity, the allegations could not legally be possible. He also requested a jury trial. This was the first salvo in what was expected to be a long war.

It was several days later when my lawyer showed up at my house. "Roger, I've got some important stuff to go over. Can we talk?"

"Of course," I said, showing him to my study. "Want some coffee?"

"Nah."

He took a seat and spread out his papers on my desk. "Okay, Roger, we have some decisions to make. First, as we discussed last week, if we fight this case and lose, you're facing ten years in prison from the Coryell County's charges and another ten years from Hamilton County *if* they indict you. Keep in mind a judge could stack the sentences, so you'd have to serve them consecutively. You're almost seventy years old. I don't have to do the math for you or explain how poorly cops do in prison. Their life expectancy is not good."

I shifted uncomfortably in my chair. "Thanks for the pep talk, buddy. Any good news for me?"

Tim coughed. "This is going to be a long fight. Here's what it will cost to defend you on all this so far." He slid a piece of paper over.

I felt a pain in my forehead, rubbing it for half a minute. "Tim, this is going to ruin me financially. Mary and I will be out on the street."

"Look, that figure includes a healthy budget for a private detective and a forensic expert to look at Bobo's electronic devices. We'll also have to check the other elected officials' devices—legally, of course—along with Alexander's and that person known to you. Something is going on around here and we'll have to get to the bottom of it. It's the only way to ensure victory in your case. Otherwise, a jury can be a crapshoot. You know that. You've seen many a guilty criminal go free while innocent people are locked up only to be let out twenty years later when DNA clears them."

I took in a deep breath and closed my eyes. "Continue, please."

"The good news is I talked to both the district attorney and county attorney and received a special offer today. It's like one of those two-for-one specials they have at your previously favorite western wear store. Are you ready for this?"

"I guess," I said in a low voice.

Tim leaned back and smiled. "They'll drop all charges against you right now if you'll resign from being constable."

"What else?"

"That's it!"

"Can I run for sheriff?"

"You can run for sheriff, governor, senator, whatever you want. They just want your constable's position for some reason."

"Why?"

"I have no idea."

"Tim, this doesn't make sense. All my troubles will be over if I just resign my poorly paid position? I'm supposed to be this big-time criminal. Why would they let me run for sheriff if I was such a dirty cop?"

"Again, I don't know. But why do you care? Let's take this deal before the aliens leave their bodies and we're back to dealing with the real lawyers."

I sat there for a while in silence, pondering his words. "I need to think about this, pray about it."

"There's no time. We need to book this deal now or it's gone. They're putting on the pressure."

"Let me lay this out. I can win, but I'll be broke. I can lose, go to prison, and be broke. Or I simply resign my eighteen-thousand-dollar-per-year job and everything's good. I can keep my money, my ranch, my fencing business, and be sheriff one day."

Tim nodded his head. I leaned back in my chair, holding the figure he'd given me. Lawyers and litigation were so incredibly expensive. No wonder so many innocent people went to prison.

Tim was a great lawyer, a fighter. I knew I wanted to fight. But spending the money meant Mary would have to suffer. And giving up a job that actually *cost* me money seemed like a no-brainer. I could make more money in my fencing business by *not* being constable. Even though I was sure I could win these cases, if my lawyer made one tiny mistake or I got Tommy Haggerty or Scott Williams on the jury, I'd be ninety when I got out of prison. No rational human being could make any other decision.

"Tim, when you get over there, tell them that I have so much respect for my badge, I'm going to retire. I'll take their deal. But if they try to pull something, I'll fight them all the way. I'm not going to drag my badge through any kind of bullshit."

"I'll tell them, Roger."

I waited for him to get back to me. It took almost a week. When we reconnected, he had a huge smile on his face. "I got the deal done. And I also got some information that proves this was a setup."

"What kind of information?" I asked.

He handed me a document. It was a letter dated January 15, 2015, talking about me and charges relating to official oppression, tampering/fabricating evidence, and false statement to a peace officer. The only problem was that I didn't go out to the property until two months later—March 2015. So how could they have decided I'd be charged with those crimes two months *before* anything happened?

I could hardly believe what I was reading. The document was official. It had the Coryell County District Attorney's letterhead at the top. And it was signed by the Coryell District Attorney *and* the County Attorney. The two Coryell County lawyers had authenticated this document with their signatures. Before I asked Tim about it, he showed me the dismissal of the criminal charges and the nonsuit to my removal suit. They even had Hamilton County give up any right to file charges on me. It seemed like everyone was good friends with Coryell County when it came to prosecuting me.

Despite this new evidence, I had already taken the deal. As promised, I resigned as constable. And sure enough, they had someone selected to take my job.

I kept looking for the missing backhoe, certain it would lead to something big. But before I got too far, the local paper ran my mug shot on the front page, saying I'd resigned. They wanted to get their last licks in. But I wasn't stopping. As a private citizen, I could still ask around about that backhoe.

One day, I was running down leads when the very man who had taken my elected position sent me a letter. He had filed a case to have me dishonorably discharged as a peace officer. As with Sheriff Burks, I confronted him. He admitted he had not investigated anything and didn't feel he had to. A few days later, the matter was dropped, and I was *not* dishonorably discharged. I still kept my peace officer's license.

It seemed like whenever I pressed on the backhoe, a fist came out of nowhere and punched me in the face.

Coincidence?

Strange?

You decide, because that's the way it was.

THE WAY IT WAS

Coryell County Sheriff John W. Hammack administers the ultimate
punishment to Leeper and Powell.

Roger's first caribou since arriving in Alaska.
The location is the Bonanza Hills.

HAMMACK, REX LOY

SF 3/c Rex Loy Hammack, son of Mr. and Mrs. Wesley Hammack, Ireland, husband of Ernestine Tippie, Hamilton, attended Ireland and Aleman schools. Entered Navy, 1943, served in EAME and Pacific. Awarded ET Ribbon, 4 Battle Stars, Pres. Citation, and GCM. Discharged in 1945.

Roger's father, Rex, and his World War II service record.

Roger's daughter, Heather, holding a 65-pound salmon. She caught two salmon that day with a total weight over 100 pounds. This photo is in the front yard of Roger's house in Soldotna, Alaska, just 100 yards from the Kenai River.

Roger with his airplane on a bear hunt with Roland.

Roger and Roland's guide camp in the Wrangel Mountains.

Roland removes walrus tusks in Alaska. The walrus had died in the
ocean and washed up, the only legal way to take the tusks. At the time,
the tusks were number three in Boone and Crockett record book.

Roger's father, Rex, holds a fish he caught on the Kenai River as
Roger's daughter, Heather, looks on.

Roger with a brown bear on Alaska's Unimak Island.

Roland and Roger's mother with moose antlers. Roland shot the Boone and Crockett record at the Hammack's guide camp in the Wrangel Mountains.

Roger with his first grandson and first deputy, Roger.

Roger in Wyoming with a mule deer.

Poker Nights. (*seated l to r*) Jimmy Payne, Rusty Lilliedahl, James Kruse, Roger Schwalbe. (*standing l to r*) Bobby Hammack, Jimmy Tabor, Tommy McKay.

Roger's daughter Regina with her husband, Ron King.

Roland and Roger with a client's moose antlers at their camp in
Wrangle Mountains

Roger's fencing and ranch crew.
(*front row l to r*) Johna (Shorty) Schumann, Trish Butler, Michael Harley, Christian Casselman. (*back row l to r*) Ronnie Hammack, Jimmy Neylund, Matt Harley, Willis Holden, Terry Haney.

Roger and Ronnie and his mule in a Gatesville's Fourth of July parade.

Roger's client, Justin Tatum, stands in front of his family's refurbished cabin originally built in 1880.

Poker Nights Two.
(*l to r*) David Truss, Dale Adkins, Denver Tippit, John Young, Jack Morse, Bob Gardner, Steve Young, Justin Saunders, Darren Poe.

Roger with his grandson, Andrew Gilbert, in Wyoming. They have been hunting there each year since Andrew was five years old, when Andrew bagged his first mule deer.

Roger at Lake Fork with his great friend attorney Tim Tesch.

Four-Star General Benjamin S. Griffin with Roger leaning on a fence Roger built for the Texas Cattlemen's Association next to Fort Hood.

Roger with his son, Warren, and grandson, Roger, in Wyoming.

Poker Nights Three. (*l to r*) Brian Stazza, Ernestine Coplen, Floyd Coplen, Wilfred Van Note, Karen Woody, Mark Lam, Cody Smith.

Roger with a Dall sheep taken in Alaska's Wrangel Mountains.

Lance Horn, a young kid who started working for Roger as a
sophomore in high school, bagged a mule deer in Wyoming.
Roger takes Lance hunting every chance he has.

The kids of Springbox Farms enjoy their new petting zoo.

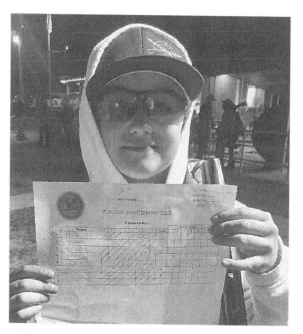

Rowan Hammack, Roger's grandson, holding his score sheet for competition skeet shooting."

Poker Nights Four. (*l to r*) Ernestine Coplen, Geneva Moore, Jimmy Wilcox, Karen Woody, Mark Carr, Brian Stazza, Jack Johnson, Tim Tesch, Randy Tesch, Unknown, Floyd Coplen, Bobby Hammack.

EPILOGUE

If someone walked up to you on the street and said, "Our elected law enforcement officer has been indicted for a felony in one county and will likely be indicted for a second felony in another county. We've sued to remove him from office. He's a dirty cop," would you have any reason to doubt this was the truth? I wouldn't.

But what if, a few weeks later, that same person told you that this dirty cop's charges had been dismissed once he agreed to resign? What if they told you he's still allowed to run for any public office, including sheriff? And, to top it all off, his badge hasn't been revoked?

If you'd just heard all that, would you still think the cop was dirty? I wouldn't. I'd think someone just wanted him out of office for some reason.

That's why, when I spotted the man who'd filed the dishonorable discharge request against me, I just had to ask him a question. "Why didn't you come and ask me questions? Didn't you think it was proper to hear my side before you filed your request?"

The newly appointed constable gave me a glare. "Why in the hell should I ask you anything?"

"Because you want to get to the truth of the matter. Remember that word? It's an important one. Truth!"

He gave me the evil eye and left, taking my elected position with him.

Once again, I couldn't believe the sheer ignorance. File, but don't investigate. Indict, but don't ask for the other side. It never changed.

Several months after all this, I decided to run for my old job again—constable. I had been hurt badly by all the lies, and needed to get my good reputation back. One day, I was talking to some people about that missing backhoe and received a call from my lawyer.

"You must be stirring the pot again," he said. "I just received a letter from the district attorney saying they are going to indict you if you run for constable. But I think you can legally run since it wasn't part of our deal."

"I understand," I replied.

"Are you still going to run?" he asked me.

"Yes, and I'm going to find out who has that backhoe. Then we'll discover who's behind all this."

The threats increased, but I was never indicted. However, the mug shots that ran in the newspaper surely affected me. I lost the election. But I knew I was going to run for another office like the Sheriff of Coryell County one day. I just needed to learn why someone didn't want me looking for stolen property.

I continued checking into the investigation of my case. In July 2018, I called the Texas Rangers in Waco. I asked for the major and he wasn't in. They suggested the lieutenant, but he was busy. With no one available to talk to me, I left a message.

I waited and waited, but the lieutenant never called me. After an appropriate time, I called him again and finally got through. I told him who I was and that Ranger Bobo had investigated me. I explained how I'd been indicted on false allegations and said, "If you would just read his reports and let me tell you my side of the story—"

"I don't have to read Ranger Bobo's reports, because he's the most efficient Ranger we have," he said, cutting me off. "You need to go to the district attorney."

This was strange, because normally when a citizen—in this case, a current Texas peace officer and former elected official—called and raised issues about a case, any professional law enforcement officer would look into them.

I told him the district attorney didn't want to be involved, and that was the end of our conversation. Still, I wasn't giving up.

About three weeks passed and I went to DPS, telling the sergeant there that I needed to talk to the colonel. I told him the whole story in private. When I was done, he wrote down a name: Lt. Col. Randall Prince. I asked if that was Bobby Prince's son—the one who had been shot with a BB gun when he was just a kid. Bobby and I had rounded up the punks and "resolved" the matter. The sergeant said it might be Bobby's son, but he wasn't sure.

Finally, I was getting somewhere. I knew without a doubt that Bobby Prince would've passed down his first-class genes to his son. If there was someone who would finally listen, Lt. Col. Randall Prince was it.

I called the phone number and Lt. Col. Randall Prince wasn't available. I left a message for him to call me. After a week with no callback, I called again. I didn't get Lt. Col. Randall Prince and was transferred away from his office to another Texas Ranger's office. I told this Ranger the story, and he told me to go through the chain of command.

"Look," I told the Ranger, "I've gone as far as I can."

"Well, you need to talk to the major in Waco."

"But I called the lieutenant in Waco and got nowhere."

He insisted I call the major.

I did, but he wasn't available, so I left a message.

I waited a few weeks and had not received a call. So I called the major again, leaving another message.

A few weeks later, I repeated all this. In fact, I've been repeating this cycle for months with no callback. (As of the publication of this book, they still haven't returned my calls.) I'm guessing they're out looking for that missing backhoe. Either that, or they don't want to talk to me.

Strange.

After I suffered through this horrendous event, I threatened to sue for the harm they caused me. That would mean the citizens of Coryell County would pay any damages I might win. With my family's background and heritage, I simply couldn't do that.

After the statute of limitations had run on my civil claim, Dusty Boyd, the District Attorney, allowed me to tell another grand jury what happened to me. Because he had already dismissed the criminal charge against me, the grand jury took no action. However, I am grateful to Dusty Boyd for allowing me to tell my story.

Each year, all Texas peace officers must attend class to keep our licenses active. Recently, I called the Coryell County Sheriff's Office to talk to the coordinator of the schools, who was taking the registration. There was a class being put on at the Gatesville Civic Center by the Combined Law Enforcement Agencies of Texas (CLEAT). It was free and I wanted to register for it. Thirty minutes after I talked to the coordinator, Sheriff Scott Williams called me.

"What can I do for you, Mr. Hammack?" he said dramatically, his voice dripping with controlled anger.

"I called down there to talk to your coordinator about attending that class in Gatesville," I explained.

"Well, that's just for my employees," he said.

I knew that was a blatant lie. I'd heard about the class from a Hamilton City police officer who'd said he was attending. And I knew the very name CLEAT involved multiple law enforcement agencies. Why he would lie about something as simple as that, I had no idea.

"You're the boss," I replied, trying to de-escalate things.

"Yep," he snapped, "I'm the boss."

A silence fell between us. He spoke first.

"What's this I hear about you going around telling everyone how much of a liar I am, and that you're going to run for sheriff? I also hear that you're writing a book."

"Yes, that's true on all three counts," I told him.

"You're getting in way over your head. You don't know what you're getting into. You'd better stop it right now!" he barked at me, his voice rising to the level of the Western Wear store incident.

I took this to mean a threat to my personal safety, as in bodily harm. I said nothing.

"I want the first copy—to give to my lawyer!" Scott demanded.

I took this to be a threat of a civil lawsuit. With a chuckle, I answered, "I'll save the first copy for you. And I'll even autograph it for you."

We ended the conversation on a high note, mainly because I was still alive. I decided it was wise not to attend the class, even though I knew full well I could go. Coryell County has a lot of dark dirt roads. No telling when a man can be pulled over and someone jerks a gun from their holster, accidentally putting a round or ten into his chest. I'd have to be satisfied with obtaining the attendees' list from CLEAT to see if it had more than the sheriff's department members there, and if Scott Williams had lied to a fellow law enforcement officer.

The very next day after Scott's call, something interesting happened. I drive a special pickup when handling fencing jobs. As my pickup drove to a job, a sheriff's patrol pickup was headed in the opposite direction. The patrol pickup did a U-turn and pulled over my truck. As the patrol pickup stopped behind my truck, two law enforcement officers got out: Sheriff Scott Williams and his chief deputy. From my experience, when two men of this level are in the same vehicle, they're looking for someone. And again, from my past experience, it won't be a pleasant outcome when they find whoever they are looking for.

Unfortunately for Scott, this was one of the rare occasions that I wasn't in my pickup. I had a crew of men and women in there. None of them were killed, but I wondered what would've happened if I'd been in that truck alone.

To get my TCLOSE certification, I was forced to drive to Del Rio and check into a hotel. I spent close to $500 due to Scott's snub. I hope he got his money's worth. At least no one put Mace in my food.

In closing, as I went through this mess, I remembered something Chief Banks had said when he talked about dirty cops: "I've learned that the people who set you up usually die a slow and painful death. For the folks who lie against you, that's their just reward from the great lawman in the sky."

I don't know what will happen, but I know when I'm at the end, I'll have a clear conscience to go with my chipped tooth. The dirty cops, whoever they are, will remember their shame 'til the day they die. And when they're lying on their deathbeds, I hope my book is right there beside them.

ACKNOWLEDGMENTS

My mother, Ernestine Rebecca Hammack, was a wonderful mother, grandmother, great-grandmother, and great-great-grandmother. A loyal member of the Golf Course Road Church of Christ, she enjoyed sewing, making dolls and children's clothing, and giving out gifts. She also loved gardening her geraniums and feeding all the birds in the neighborhood.

Mother left a legacy with her family, teaching them so much through her great strength. That's why I'd never forgive myself if I didn't mention in my book that she published two books: *Tangled Deceptions* and *Somewhere Out There*. As an avid reader, she had so many stories floating around in her mind that she just had to get them down on paper. She died November 11, 2008, and has been sorely missed.

It would be very hard for me to write a book without mentioning a very special former county attorney of Coryell County—Edwin Powell. He approached me one day in the office and said, "Roger, I hear you've been helping out people around here. I'm real proud of you. If there is any way I can be of assistance attorney-wise, just let me know."

"I'm glad you brought that up," I replied. "A person I know is in a very abusive relationship. She needs to get a divorce. She has no money. If you'll handle the paperwork, I'll handle the expenses of getting the papers served. I'll even serve the papers myself."

"Oh, you bet!" he said.

I had the woman meet with Edwin and he took care of it. Months later, she was divorced and away from that violent situation.

Edwin helped on some other matters, whenever I pointed out people in need. I was grateful to be able to call him a friend. He passed away suddenly and is greatly missed.

I have to give a shout-out to my poker-playing buddies—Jimmy Payne, Rusty Lilliedahl, James Kruse, Roger Schwalbe, Bobby Hammack, Jimmy Tabor, Tommy McKay, David Truss, Dale Adkins, Denver Tippit, John Young, Jack Morse, Bob Gardner, Steve Young, Justin Saunders, Darren Poe, Brian Stazza, Ernestine Coplen, Floyd Coplen, Wilfred Van Note, Karen Woody, Mark Carr, Cody Smith, Geneva Moore, Jimmy Wilcox, Jack Johnson, Tim Tesch, and Randy Tesch. These people are bankers, wardens, coaches, homebuilders, and retired schoolteachers. We enjoy getting together to play penny ante poker, eating junk food, drinking sodas, and talking about what's going on. It's a fun way to end the week.

I once saw a bumper sticker that read: *God made all the critters and then He made ranchers to take care of them.* These are some of the men and women He had in mind:

Denver Tippit

Dale Tippit

Gene and Gary Clarke

Mark Carouthers

Crockett Carouthers

Patsy and John Miller. They're the owners of Big Creek Construction, which builds highways all over Texas. When John is gone, Patsy will sneak out there and feed the feral hogs. John will be forced to hire someone to come in and clean the hogs out.

Jim Taylor in Turnersville. Jim raises some of the best white-tailed deer in the country.

Bill Dudark. I built a game fence for Bill, and now he has one of the best hunting ranches around.

Shirley Thomas. She ran a ranch by herself as good as any man. She passed away a few years ago and her daughter Becky now runs the ranch.

Johnny Arnold. I purchased my ranch from him. Johnny is one of the hardest working people I know today. He has one of the largest cattle operations in the state.

Charles Graham. He is a large rancher in Coryell County and the state of Texas. I don't know who has the most cattle: him or Johnny Arnold.

Rick Harp. He owns a ranch with a special breeding program for white-tailed deer and other exotics.

Carla and Steve Manning. They are solid business and ranch owners. They do a lot of work on Fort Hood.

Chris Bergman. He's a great rancher and president of First National Bank. It's always good to know someone with lots of money... in the bank.

The names above are but a few of the great people I place in this category. They are tremendous assets to Coryell County and the state of Texas. They are also my good friends.

As I stated before, my great-grandfather settled in Hamilton County in the 1800s. He owned about 1,000 acres of land and raised cattle. He was well known in the area for having several cattle drives start from his ranch. About five years ago, I received a call from a man who wanted to build a fence in Ireland, Texas. I drove to his ranch and met William Lesjak and his wife, Neta. This was the ranch Daniel Leroy (my great-grandfather) had settled on in the 1800s.

We talked for a while. I learned that Neta had been born in Hamilton and raised on a ranch in Purmela, Texas. Both had retired after thirty years of working for the federal government. They are wonderful people and have taken very good care of the ranch. My family would be very proud of them. With the first handshake, we became fast friends. I will always consider them as such.

Recently, we had a tornado that came through the area. I grabbed my chainsaw and hit the streets, checking out any fence I had put up. I knew many of my customers had game behind those fences. Losing animals would not only be a financial loss to the customer, but stressful on the animal. And it could get hit by a vehicle, possibly killing someone. I wanted to make sure all my clients were doing good.

I came to one fence that I had built. A tree had fallen on it, creating an opening for the animals. Two men, Tim Elkins and Mason Crosby, were studying the situation when I rolled up and introduced myself. They said they'd purchased the ranch from my former customer. I didn't care. I fired up the chainsaw, helping them clear the fence free of charge. Once the tree was out of the way, we set the fence back up and everything was fine. They could clear the rest of the tree later.

A few weeks went by when I received a package in the mail. It was an NFL jersey. I turned it around and recognized the Green Bay Packers' colors. On the back was the name of the player—Mason Crosby. And he included a thank you note. I felt embarrassed that I had not known who he was when I met him. But that just goes to show you that you never know who you're going to meet on the streets of Coryell County.

AUTHOR BIO

From flying over a frozen Alaska to sweating out a night shift on the Big Spring Police Department, Roger Hammack has been there and done that. Recently, he put his years as patrol officer, under-cover agent, and crime detective to work as an elected constable of Coryell County. Today, he's a ranch operator and business owner in Gatesville, Texas. This is his first book. Roger can be reached at RogerHammackBook@gmail.com.

Made in the USA
Lexington, KY
20 December 2019